GETTING
TO
"I DO"

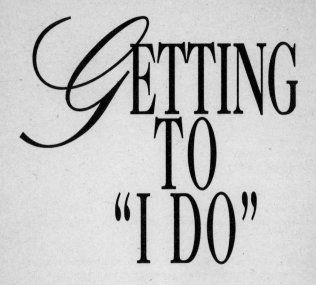

GETTING TO "I DO"

DR. PATRICIA ALLEN
and SANDRA HARMON

AVON BOOKS ▲ NEW YORK

This book is dedicated to H. P.

AVON BOOKS
A division of
The Hearst Corporation
1350 Avenue of the Americas
New York, New York 10019

Copyright © 1994 by Patricia D. Allen and Sandra Harmon
Published by arrangement with the author
Library of Congress Catalog Card Number: 93-32050
ISBN: 0-380-71815-4

Published in hardcover by William Morrow and Company, Inc.; for information address Permissions Department, William Morrow and Company, Inc., 1350 Avenue of the Americas, New York, New York 10019.

The William Morrow edition contains the following Library of Congress Cataloging in Publication Data:
Allen, Patricia, 1934-
  Getting to "I do"/ by Patricia Allen and Sandra Harmon.
    p.   cm.
1. Man-woman relationships. 2. Sex role. 3. Marriage.
I. Harmon, Sandra II. Title.
HQ801.A525   1994   93-32050
306.7—dc20   CIP

First Avon Books Trade Printing: February 1995

AVON TRADEMARK REG. U.S. PAT. OFF. AND IN OTHER COUNTRIES, MARCA REGISTRADA, HECHO EN U.S.A.

Printed in the U.S.A.

OPM 10 9 8 7 6 5 4

Foreword

The women's liberation movement changed my life. Before I read Betty Friedan's *The Feminine Mystique*, I perceived myself as a normal, middle-class, traditional Iowan wife and mother of four, who also taught art and social studies at a local junior high school. But looking back, I realize I was totally without a sense of my own rights as a human being.

My husband, a high school social studies teacher and athletic coach, whom I had married when I was nineteen and he was twenty-one, controlled every penny that we both brought home. He even did the grocery shopping. Incredible as it seems, he gave me only a quarter a day (which I kept in my loafer, because I didn't own a purse), with which I was to buy my lunch, a fifteen-cent salad—school cafeteria discount price—and a ten-cent Fresca. Most of the time, however, I used the quarter to buy stale doughnuts at a bakery thrift store near the school. The result was a steady gain in weight, until I peaked at 205 pounds.

One day a woman teacher at my school who felt sorry for me gave me a copy of *The Feminine Mystique*, which I devoured. This book made me understand that many women like myself lived under the control of much less gifted men. It also showed me how much I needed help.

I entered therapy and quickly began to bloom as an individual. I lost weight and became interested in clothes and makeup. I decided to go back to school to get my Ph.D. so I could become a psychotherapist and help others like myself.

I had hoped my husband would be proud of the changes I

was making in my life but soon discovered that independence, individuality, and good looks were not the qualities he wanted or valued in a wife. As I grew thinner, more attractive, and more able to voice my beliefs, he grew more angry and less interested in me sexually, until soon he was totally turned off.

I immersed myself in the study of human behavior. With each new class and counseling group I attended, I found myself trying to find answers to the problem of how I could successfully combine my marriage and my career. But before I could find any solutions, my husband walked out on me.

Alone for the first time in my life, I was forced to make a living, handle money, raise four daughters, finish graduate school, and begin to build a therapy practice. I was also on the lookout for a new husband, one who would accept me as I wanted to be, both married and successful.

A few months after my divorce, I met a ruggedly handsome out-of-work "cowboy," who soon asked me to marry him. My children liked him and I was thrilled to get the offer, so of course I accepted.

The first few months we were together were wonderful, except for the fact that my new husband didn't like living in my ex-husband's house with my ex-husband's furniture. So, because he was broke and I had good credit, I bought us, in order to please him, a new house, ten rooms of furniture, five thoroughbred horses, and a Harley-Davidson motorcycle.

I was thrilled when he finally got a job, but then, six months later, at a Christmas party, he got into a fight with his boss and was fired. The next day, right before I left for school, he announced he was going home to his mother's ranch. I assumed he was joking, but later that evening when I returned home, I caught what turned out to be my last glimpse of him, driving away in a large moving van with all my furniture. Naturally, he had already taken the five horses.

I never saw him, the horses, or the furniture again. A few months later, I lost my house, got high blood pressure, and had to file for bankruptcy.

I soon met another man who seemed to be just what I needed

after the "cowboy." He was loving, gentle, and rich. He didn't work because he didn't have to. He came from a fine old family and even owned a yacht. I figured he was as far away from the cowboy as I could get.

Once again, I married soon after I met my "hero," and once again, things seemed fine, at first. My husband loved me and my children, and not only did he pay all the bills, he was generous as well. Living with him made me feel secure.

But then, about a year after we married, he began to complain about feeling lonely at home while I was off pursuing my career. Although I felt guilty, knowing I did put my work ahead of our marriage, I refused to give it up. I wanted equality, just as the women's movement had promised me.

I tried hard to make the relationship work, but once again I just couldn't seem to balance my marriage and my career, and after three years we divorced.

I was beginning to wonder whether marriage and career fulfillment *were* compatible. Instead of love, equality seemed to lead to conflict and confusion.

I observed that as women got stronger and became more "male," men became intimidated and more "female," reluctant to make a commitment and take on the responsibility for an independent woman who could leave him at will. These men still wanted a traditional, controllable, docile woman, not a "woman's libber."

Certainly, most of the men I met as a single woman were either intimidated by my success or wanted me to take care of them. The rest just avoided me.

My daughters were having as much trouble as I was. As they reached maturity, they too couldn't find mates who could or would accept their having a career and the time it took away from them. Three of my daughters went to school for degrees and became professionals, while the fourth got married and had a baby. The career-oriented daughters envied the one with the husband and child, and she envied the education of the other three.

After I divorced my third husband, I stayed single for the

next eighteen years and dated a variety of men, all of whom taught me something I needed to learn.

In 1981 I earned my doctorate in psychology in the area of communication techniques. As a transactional analyst, I had studied the meaning and intent behind the words people use to communicate with one another. Soon I saw a way to simplify and package communication techniques that my clients could use easily to negotiate better relationships.

This technique, which I called Semantic Realignment and which became my doctoral dissertation, is a way to apply consistent, logical principles within a carefully worked-out system. By clarifying and applying the decision-making process, teaching individual men and women how to speak (and argue) rationally, I pragmatically established a system of complementary communication.

As an intern, I was required to run groups to demonstrate my skills. I began conducting once-a-week relationship seminars in the rec center of a local high school. My goal was to gather data and share it with as many people as I could.

Week after week, I listened to men and women who were in emotional torment over the confusion of male and female roles. I heard men complain of being smothered by women who pursued them or of feeling rejected by women who didn't. They told me that they felt thwarted from expressing their naturally "male" generosity when the woman picked up the tab. They asked what they were to do about a woman who asked them out and then expected them to pay. How were they supposed to "respect" her "male" qualities and then "cherish" her female ones as well?

Women, on the other hand, would complain of, and doubt, the manhood of men who wouldn't ask for sex. Some women refused sex until a "commitment" was made, only to see a man walk out before a relationship could be established. Other women fell in love, had sex, and expected a commitment to follow, only to find that the man had no intention of making one. On every level, there was a concern about commitment. It was clear to me that women were becoming so male that men saw them as "one of the guys" who would share money and genitals without a commitment.

There was suspicion as well. Women complained that men, with their newfound "sensitivity," talked about how they felt but were not willing to listen to how the woman felt. Whereas previously we had assumed our traditional male/female roles (males provided, females nested), we now expected everything of our mates—and consequently got little but disappointment.

It was in this setting that I began to build my relationship theories of male and female roles. Can a woman combine a career and marriage? How much independence and responsibility is good or bad in an intimate relationship?

I became fascinated by the work of Dr. Carl Jung, the brilliant Swiss analyst who believed that not only did each man and woman carry some of the hormones of the opposite sex, he or she also carried the personality characteristics of the opposite sex. He said men had a feminine side, which he called the "anima," that helped them either love or binge on women, and women had a masculine side, their "animus," that helped them to be either strong and self-loving or angry and self-destructive. Today this dualistic concept is called "androgyny."

I became determined to find out how people could balance their positive feminine and masculine sides and avoid the negative misuse of their "animus" or "anima."

Using Jung's theories as a base, I developed a theory and strategy of accommodation to help men and women balance their feminine and masculine sides in an equitable exchange that did not conflict, allowing them to share their gifts equitably as a couple. I distilled my research and passed it on to my clients in a round-robin process in therapy as well as in my weekly seminars.

Finally, I had reached my goal of assisting people in the total development of their potential—physically, mentally, and emotionally—and at the same time teaching them to communicate with each other in a way that would allow them to live lives of autonomy, creativity, and spontaneity.

Once word got around that I could actually help men and

women to communicate with each other and meet and marry successfully, the waiting rooms in my therapy offices in Los Angeles and Newport Beach, California, have rarely been empty. Too, my weekly seminars, which are now held in a large theater, are filled with standing-room-only crowds of people, many of whom are the most beautiful and successful women in Los Angeles, including some of Hollywood's brightest stars, top filmmakers, and power executives—all successful "males" in the office or on the set, yet not necessarily successful "females" in their romantic relationships. They come to my seminars, listen to my radio show, and have made my self-help tapes best-sellers. Of course, newspapers and magazines have published articles on me, calling me the "love doctor" or relationship "guru," and I have appeared on many major TV shows.

From a vantage point of twenty years, I see the results of my relationship work in the thousands of men and women who attend my seminars and experiment and explore until they have found their own way of using these teachings. They become better skilled in loving and relating. More than two thousand couples have married and stayed together through the use of my techniques.

It happened to me, too. One evening a very delightful man came to one of my seminars. He kept coming back, and we got to know each other. Over the next three years, he used the information he learned at these groups to court me. In 1990 we married.

My three single daughters, who of course at first discounted my information because I was "Mom," later used it and married wonderful men.

Now I want all of you to achieve the same fulfillment that we have. With my coauthor, Sandra Harmon, I have in this book synthesized all the research and experience of my twenty years of practice as a marriage counselor and family and child therapist and a transactional analyst.

Because mine is a new and different way of looking at relationships, my rules of behavior may anger some people. But I can't help that—the rules still work. My system is not complex, but it does answer the needs of individuals who live in a complex world. What I am advocating is that you be able to make educated choices in the areas of relationships and career, combining these to suit your own specific needs.

I wish to thank the many people who have contributed in their own way to this book.

First and foremost, I want to thank my coauthor, Sandra Harmon. Six years ago she came to one of my seminars. We met afterward and I was impressed with her dynamic, ebullient personality and brilliant mind, as well as the fact that she had coauthored Priscilla Presley's best-seller, *Elvis and Me*.

I asked Sandy if she would collaborate with me on this book, and after spending the next year studying my theories and using them in her own life, she agreed. She believed in my work, and I appreciated and needed her extraordinarily logical mind, her humor, and her skills as a great writer, interpreter, and popularizer of complex ideas. "Thank you, Sandy" hardly says it all, but it is what I want to say. Without her this book could not and would not have been written.

There have been others who have helped us along the way. Sandy's agency, William Morris, which with its top literary agent Owen Laster was a bonus for me, as an unknown author. Pam Bernstein, who worked with Owen, was wonderfully supportive, and helped us sell the book to Susan Leon and Howard Kaminsky at William Morrow. Thanks also to Liza Dawson, who became our supportive editor after Susan Leon left Morrow, and to Sally Arteseros, who did a superb job editing the final draft of this manuscript. Thanks also to Marcy Posner, who became our agent at William Morris after Pam left. I want to thank my loyal and patient husband, Guy, and my four daughters, especially Susan, for all the practical help they have given me.

I also want to thank my longtime associates Marilyn Brown, Bob Stohr, Tom Lord, Rick Harrison, Chloe Parham, and Lucille Posner, who, along with many others who have come and gone into their own practices, helped work out the kinks in my system. Thanks also to Steven Kral, who was with us at the beginning.

My special thanks, of course, to the thousands of women and men who have, through their successes and failures, helped me learn each idea, each technique, every step of the way. This book is a result of those twenty years of research with thousands of women just like me. Because of their wish to know new ways to enhance their ability to become engaged and married, they helped me compile this information from which you will benefit. As a therapist and as a woman, I owe much to these clients and students.

And, finally, I want to thank you, the reader. As long as women (and men) like you pursue better answers for life's issues by seeking books, seminars, and lectures to learn from, the human race will profit with better marriages and families.

My promise to you is that after applying the information you learn from reading this book, you will

1. Evolve and balance your masculine and feminine energy.
2. Be able to attract, observe, and evaluate your potential mate's inner balance and marriageability.
3. Have the communication skills to negotiate a sound engagement and marriage within one year.

Contents

Part Three
The Four Stages of a Relationship

Part Four
The Rest of the Story

The women's movement brought us independence, but it did not bring us love.

—DR. PATRICIA ALLEN

Introduction

This book is for any man or woman who is trying to find and/or keep a lover in the nineties, but it is primarily directed to women. There are many thousands of you out there who are successful at work but find yourselves without a relationship because you are confused by male and female roles. I will show you the clues you have been missing and why. I will tell you ten secrets that will allow you to meet the man you want and become engaged, very likely in this first year.

That successful, adorable unmarried man you see around the office or in your apartment building or at fashionable affairs—how do you get him to ask you out?

I can teach you how to attract his attention, get him to date you, begin a healthy sexual relationship, *and* become engaged, often by the end of the first year.

What about the man you've already given time, sex, and energy to for the past year or two?

I can teach you how to bring him back to life, *or* get rid of him for a better man.

If you're a powerful woman, you don't have to change. You just have to learn how to use your female side to attract men— that is, if you want to be the female in the relationship. If not, I will teach you how to get the "right" man who will respect *your* leadership.

This book offers new choices to any man or woman who wishes to achieve a stable, long-term relationship and/or marriage.

QUESTIONS THIS BOOK WILL ANSWER

What men want from women, and what women want from men . . .

Why equality doesn't work, but equity does . . .

How to tell if he is a giver or a taker . . .

How to tell if he's a woman-hater . . .

How to tell if you're a man-hater, and how to change into a man-lover . . .

Why a feminine woman shouldn't make the first move . . .

Why a feminine woman doesn't tell her masculine man what she thinks, just how she feels . . .

Why a masculine man can't fall in love when he is *with* a woman, only when he is away from her . . .

Why you should never have sex with a man until you get a commitment from him . . .

Why a feminine woman can't pursue a masculine man . . .

How to tell if you'd rather be the male in the relationship . . .

Why asking for what you want from a masculine man will get you nowhere . . .

Why you must never argue with a man . . .

How to get him to ask you to marry him in one year . . .

PART ONE

BEFORE YOU GO
OUT THE DOOR

CHAPTER 1

Does This Sound Like You?

You're alone, successful, and the clock is ticking. You're still young; you are liberated and complex. You want your brains respected and your feelings cherished by a man you respect and cherish. You want to join with this man in a partnership of thoughts, feelings, and mutual life goals—home, family, and an interesting career. You have dated men who seem right in the beginning, but then it all falls apart . . . usually within the first year. Sometimes you break free, and other times you stay too long.

You find yourself envying women with men you wouldn't want, who are mothers of unbearable kids who live in houses you hate—*why?* You think of marrying that nice, boring man your accountant fixed you up with, or the man you met in the grocery store who knew the price of every item, and suddenly you feel sick in the pit of your stomach—*why?*

You work more, hoping the money will feel good. You travel with your single/divorced women friends only to spend the time trying to catch a man. Or maybe you have a rare date with the "perfect" guy, but he just doesn't call back. You may still be with that married man who promises to leave his boring wife but never does.

You try to settle for that reasonably attractive associate professor of philosophy with the bright conversation and the clip-out coupons for two-for-one dinners, but you just can't. *Why?*

WHY PEOPLE AREN'T GETTING AND STAYING MARRIED

Dr. Carl Jung said that every man has a feminine, feeling side, and every woman has a masculine, thinking side, but until the 1960s, men who had to go out into the world to become "bread-winners" repressed their feminine side, while women who married and became "homemakers" repressed their masculine side. In those days, traditional values still prevailed in dating, courtship, and marriage. Premarital sex was frightening be-cause of the risk of pregnancy. Abortions were illegal, danger-ous, and inaccessible to many. Divorce was still a scandal, and good women obeyed their husbands.

But in the early 1970s, the feminist movement communicated for the first time on a mass scale that "maleness," or the male qualities that represented success, was something that could be actively pursued by women. Money, power, independence, and prestige were all within a woman's grasp and for the first time represented something that could be realistically achieved without sacrificing cultural values. What was sacrificed were the traditional roles of male and female that had for generations been the foundation of successful relationships. In fact, women became ashamed—and understandably so, given their new ac-culturation—of being satisfied with the traditional female role.

Instead of just becoming "housewives," secretaries, or teach-ers, women also became managers, lawyers, college professors, and corporation presidents, just as men, not coincidentally, be-gan releasing a more loving, gentle, and sensitive side of their nature. In Jungian terms, both women and men had begun to develop both sides of their true selves, the masculine as well as the feminine.

Soon there were no rules of behavior particular to the male or the female in a romantic relationship. He could call her, or she could call him. She could pay for the date, or he could, or they could split it. He could pursue her, or she could pursue him. She could initiate sex, or he could. Free love was in. Com-

mitment was out. Equality was the name of the game! Soon relationships became a kind of battleground on which men and
women sought equal status, equal degrees of power and prestige.

If this were restricted to the boardroom, it would represent
only a broadening of the field of combat—but, not surprisingly,
it entered the bedroom as well. With both men and women
vying for the same position, the courtship dance was abandoned to two partners struggling for the lead. In the process,
we forgot how to make love to one another.

Then, with the onset of AIDS, things changed again. Free
love was out; sexual responsibility was in. Commitment, monogamy, stability, and marriage became more desired and valued. Women began to realize that it wasn't just sex and success
they wanted; they yearned for a husband and children—in
other words, a family. But how were they to find it? Few knew
how to get into a relationship, much less stay in one.

Grim statistics tell us that a small percentage of women over
thirty will marry. Exactly half the marriages that are performed
are doomed to end in divorce. What is almost as bad is the
number of relationships that self-destruct before ever reaching
the altar, before ever having the chance to beat those odds.

But *you* can beat the odds.

DO YOU WANT IT ALL, OR ARE YOU WILLING
TO COMPROMISE TO GET HIM?

Freud, at the end of his career, asked the question "What do
women want?" The answer most appropriate today is "everything," and that is exactly what is wrong. Women (and men)
who want it all end up with nobody to love.

In today's society, healthy men and women are so ambisexual, so fully both male and female, that they seem not to need
each other anymore. Women can earn a living and live alone;
men can cook and live alone. Nobody has to get married to
have sex. Serial monogamy, which is a series of short-term,

monogamous romances, is now the major relating formula of the day, and narcissism the predominant personality disorder.

There is nothing wrong with healthy narcissism, because it means that each of us has the right to be a total person, with both male and female qualities. We each have the right to think and to feel. We each have a right to our own body. We have the right to be an individual, separate from all others. So we have advanced to the place where we can be all by ourselves if we want to be. The problem is, how do we get together?

There are now four people in every relationship instead of just two—his male and his female, and her female and her male—four complex creatures who want the freedom to be respected for their thinking and cherished for their feelings, often at the same time. But equality tends to be competitive. Nobody in an "equal" relationship wants to give up his or her rights.

But in romance, only opposites attract. People who are similar repel one another. What is "romance"? For women, romance means fantasizing that a man cares so much about her that he feels responsible for her and will protect her, be generous to her, and take care of her feelings. He acts like "her man."

The other side of the deal is that even though she is as smart as he is, she will listen to his ideas, defer to his thinking, not challenge him, and not make him prove himself or make him feel inadequate. She becomes "his woman." That is the trade-off, and it works. It's "equity" instead of "equality."

These days, marriage is seen as an "equal" partnership, but romantic relationships are not joint ventures between company presidents. They are a corporate structure including one president, who is in charge of ideas and plans (the male energy), and one vice president, in charge of feelings and veto rights (the female energy).

The male president brings the status and security and is in charge of the material portion of the relationship: money, property, work; the female vice president brings the sensuousness and sexuality and is in charge of the abstract spiritual level. While the female has ultimate veto power over the material level, she usually does it his way.

When you negotiate a relationship, you exchange commodity goods. If you want marital status and money (male), then you'd better have enough sensuous skills to exchange for his money and status. If you want sensuality and sexuality (female), then you'd better be willing to come up with the money and status.

So you must choose to be either the male *or* the female energy. It doesn't matter whether the man or the woman assumes the male or female role, as long as there is only one of each.

Once you choose whether you want to be the female or the male energy, you must learn how to find a man, attract him to you, and begin a relationship that will last. You need to follow simple, consistent, comprehensive rules of behavior that will take you from the first moment of chemical attraction through commitment and beyond.

If you choose to be the "female" energy, you must learn to dress and behave in a "feminine" way so you can attract a "masculine" man and begin a healthy and lasting relationship. If with your "female" energy you hook up with a "feminine-energy" man instead, you will both be waiting for the other to take the lead.

If, however, you choose to be the "male" energy in a relationship, you must look for a "feminine energy" man to complement you because you will collide with a masculine man instead of negotiating a commitment.

A woman can be masculine without castrating a man or feminine without denying her own personality. The women's movement freed us all to become whatever we want to be. Now we can attain any type of romantic relationship we desire, not based on our genitals, but on our own personal yearnings.

I am not attempting to teach men how to be men and women how to be women. This isn't *The Total Woman*, or *The Total Man*. It is a guide to help you select your style based on your own choice of masculine or feminine energy. And it's not absolute. Eventually, you and your mate can negotiate changes in various aspects of your male and female roles as various needs or desires arise.

When women are condemned to sacrificial femininity and are not allowed to think for themselves, the capabilities of their own minds are diminished. When men are condemned to sacrificial masculinity in which their feelings are not considered, they are being used as money and sex machines.

I will illustrate how male energy gives first, and how female energy gives back, to reward male energy.

Each person can bring either male or female energy to the relationship. The important thing is to know what you are comfortable with, and to pick a mate who complements you.

WHAT IS MALE AND WHAT IS FEMALE?

Western culture has traditionally cast men as the protectors, leaders, and predominant doers. Men have traditionally proposed to women, have conferred status upon women, and have been the security providers.

Women, on the other hand, have been the domesticators, the followers, the recipients—they have made themselves available to the life plans of men, responsive to male needs until their own separate needs for status and security began to emerge.

Maleness, in these terms, is the pragmatic, functional way in which we handle work, the initiator of action. It is the verbal, the left lobe of the brain.

Femaleness is the passive, the receptive, the emotional; it can be represented by nonverbal energy. Its function in traditional terms is to serve as an outlet for emotion and as a moral brake; it can be seen as the stable center that allows a relationship to develop and be maintained.

Although both male and female elements are vital to the makeup of both men and women, I believe that for a relationship to be healthy and successful these must be reconciled and become complementary to each other. In other words, there can only be one male and one female in every relationship.

Which would you rather be?

A SUCCESSFUL RELATIONSHIP

As I have said, the first thing you must do is choose to be the male or female energy and find a mate who complements you. Then you must learn how to build a successful relationship.

A successful relationship has three components: chemistry, compatibility, and communication.

Chemistry is lust, that immediate attraction to one another. You can't do anything about chemistry. You're either attracted to someone or you're not.

Compatibility is how much you both like each other, and that often involves sharing common interests, enjoying the same things, having the same goals.

Communication includes verbal as well as emotional communication, sex and affection as well as spiritual communication. Communication is the key to intimacy in any situation. When problems arise in communication, negotiations and intimacy fail and give way to intimidation and seduction.

I have found that in relationships, every three months or so a crisis erupts that spins the relationship significantly forward or backward. Because of this, the first year of every relationship has four distinct phases, almost like the changes in seasons:

1. The Perfect Phase is the first three months. If this phase were a season, it would be summer, when you feel warm and malleable toward each other. The chemical attraction is strong between the two of you. You both look right to one another, dress right, talk right, and your manners are correct. Everything is perfect. You have met your ideal mate.

2. The Imperfect Phase occurs during the second three months. This period is a bit like autumn, when things start to cool down. People who have a fear of intimacy, the Ninety-Day Wonders, as I call them, usually like to abort the relationship between the third and sixth month. As soon as the Perfect Period is over, these people run off to again seek the perfect person.

3. The third three months make up the Negotiable Phase, when you and your prince face the cold, hard facts about each other and decide whether or not you can accept the other's faults and adjust to the problems within the relationship. If you find you are more compatible than incompatible, that you like each other more than not, you will begin to negotiate a commitment.

There are four primary areas in which you negotiate:

(a) Money: mine, yours, and ours. How do we handle it, and who does the handling?
(b) Space: Should we live at your place, my place, or (as I suggest) separately until engaged or married? How do we handle big maintenance items and chores between us?
(c) Time: "my," "your," and "our" time. How do we allocate each?
(d) Play: What activities do "I" want to do without you, and what activities do "we" want to do together? What activities do we want to do with others?

Flexibility in role behavior is the mode of this period. Each person is "coming out" more uniquely than in the earlier phases of the relationship, so this is the time when you begin to negotiate an interchanging of masculine and feminine roles, based on each partner's personal preference.

4. The Commitment Phase is the last three-month phase. Like a new spring, this period provides new life to the relationship and is a foundation for permanence. It is at this time that you negotiate a long-term commitment, usually involving marriage.

In essence, this book covers that dramatic first year in a relationship, so that when you say, "We met in May, now it's the first of August, and we've just had our first fight," I want you to know what lies ahead and what to watch for, so that the relationship isn't derailed.

CHAPTER 2

The Story of Two Women

LESLIE

Leslie Marshall, a beautiful blonde with a great figure, wearing a sexy black cocktail dress, was getting ready to leave a charity dinner dance when she noticed a well-dressed man with the sensuous good looks that had always attracted her walk through the door.

Leslie, a dynamic account executive at a small advertising agency, was eager for a relationship. She had a wonderful job, good friends, great clothes, even her own condo. But the one thing missing from her life was a husband. She couldn't understand why, although she'd been with many, men all seemed to want sex but not commitment.

Now Leslie wanted very much to connect with this handsome stranger, so believing it perfectly acceptable to pursue a man the same way he might pursue her, she crossed the room, and with a broad smile introduced herself and asked him to dance.

He accepted, and on the dance floor Leslie learned that he was a computer consultant named Mark who had a terrific sense of humor, held her close, danced beautifully, and turned her on.

One hour later Leslie and Mark left the party and went to his apartment, where they barely made it into his bedroom before they began making love.

A modern woman, Leslie enjoyed sex and believed in getting it out of the way early. She worried about AIDS, of course, and always protected herself, but usually when she was attracted to someone, like Mark, she didn't hold back.

Mark was a wonderful lover, enduring and eager to satisfy her. By the next morning, Leslie was sure she was in love with this smart, sexy, gentle, and sensitive man.

Mark and Leslie's courtship began that night, in a style that seems typical of today's world. They were both articulate people who believed in equality in romantic relationships. They both wanted the freedom to call each other, to plan dates, to seek the other's business and financial counsel, and to share painful feelings openly. They believed that men could display their sensitivity and still be respectable, and that women could be successful and smart and still be desirable and lovable.

So what went wrong?

Leslie was a "giving" woman. If Mark had a personal or business problem, Leslie would stay up, talking well into the night, trying to help him solve it, even though she had to get up early and go to her own office the next day. If he complained of a headache, she would rub his neck and sometimes throw in a full-body massage. She even tried to help him save money, and when his car was in the shop for repairs, she gave him hers so that he didn't have to rent one, even though this limited her mobility, took time away from her business, her aerobics classes, and her friends.

Mark thought he had struck gold. He loved the fact that Leslie was not only beautiful, powerful, willing, and sexual, *but also* nondemanding, self-sufficient, and self-motivated. He respected her ability to run a business during the day and still provide a nurturing, loving environment after work.

Did Leslie occasionally feel a twinge of resentment about how much she was putting out without getting much back? Well, yes, but still she never told Mark how she really felt and never let him reciprocate, even when he offered, because she feared that he would be inconvenienced or annoyed doing things for her that she could do for herself. Leslie wanted to be totally self-sufficient, a low-maintenance woman, so that Mark would never resent her as a burden and leave, as so many others had.

About four months into the relationship, Leslie learned that a close friend had died suddenly. That night when Mark came over, he found her in her bedroom crying. She told him what had happened, then flung herself into his arms, expecting him to comfort her the way she always comforted him. Instead of holding her close and rocking her in his arms, he began talking about a problem he was having with a broker in his office.

But Leslie couldn't help Mark because she was distraught and needed him to help her. They began to snap at each other, and soon their angry words escalated into a fight. Leslie found herself losing control in a way she had never done before.

"Goddamn you, Mark," she said. "Don't you care about anyone but yourself? My friend is dead and all you think about is your career."

Mark felt his anger rising as well but tried to hold it back. "Listen, Leslie," he said calmly. "I'm really sorry about your friend, and I understand how bad you feel, but there's nothing we can do about it tonight. On the other hand, my problem's got to be solved by morning."

Leslie couldn't believe what she was hearing. "I never ask you for anything," she cried. "I always take care of myself. Why can't you give back to me when I need you?"

Mark's face turned dark. "So you have a scorecard on me, do you? You think I owe you something? Well, I have news for you. I will not be controlled by guilt over what you do for me. I will not be manipulated by you or any other woman."

A moment later, Mark slammed the door and was out of her apartment as Leslie stood, rooted to the spot, shocked by how quickly things had fallen apart. She tried to run after him, but when she reached her apartment house lobby, Mark was already gone. Leslie watched the clock for fifteen minutes, then called him. There was no answer. She called again. All that night she called, but he never picked up the phone.

Early the next morning, Leslie was back on the phone trying to reach Mark, but there was still no answer. She finally reached him at work; he icily listened to her awkward apology and agreed to come over that evening.

That night, Leslie was on her best behavior, solicitous of Mark's every need. As they made love, she did not even think of her needs (nor did he) and pushed down her feelings of neglect. She was willing to put his feelings ahead of her own. Mark was the best man she had ever had, and she didn't want to lose him.

But after that night, there was a subtle distance between them. One night when Leslie tried to initiate sex, Mark angrily told her that he wasn't about to become a sex machine for her pleasure. Another time when plans Leslie had made for the two of them coincided with something else that Mark wanted to do, he accused her of trying to control him. Then, when Leslie was describing her handling of a certain business situation, Mark's strenuous criticism of it turned into an argument when she accused him of trying to boss her around.

Things would get better, then worse. Mark stopped calling as often as he had in the past, and she was so confused and miserable that she started calling him more, only to hear a coolness in his voice that made her feel as if she were intruding.

Leslie tried everything she could think of to bring back the relationship. She read self-help books, listened to talk shows, and sought out the counsel of friends, but nowhere did she find an answer to keep from losing Mark.

Daily, she felt herself slipping into the pathetic woman she never wanted to be. Abandonment and fear were becoming problems that constantly pushed her into giving more and asking for reassurance, but Mark responded only by laughing or changing the subject. The more she chased after him, the more he pulled away. The nights she did get him to agree to see her seemed to end in emotional outbursts, in jealousy and fear that he was seeing another woman, all those issues that she knew would drive him away.

Leslie knew she had an obsession when she found herself driving by his house, watching beautiful women coming and going, women who seemed perfect in comparison to her. Then, suddenly, her despair turned to rage, and all she wanted to do was to hurt him.

One night, after begging him to see her and having him refuse, she went to his apartment and knocked on his door. After a long wait, Mark came to the door, clad only in a robe. It was obvious to Leslie that he had been in bed with someone else.

When he wouldn't let her in, Leslie started screaming. "You have someone in there, don't you?" She clawed her way past him as he tried to hold her back. She made it as far as his bedroom where she saw a frightened woman in his bed, holding a blanket in front of her.

Mark managed to push Leslie out of his apartment. Shrieking, she ran to her car, started it, and drove off wildly, but then she stopped and cried on the steering wheel, whimpering like a small child. Miserable and depressed, she at last knew the relationship was over.

For weeks Leslie could barely leave her home. She mostly stayed in bed, watching TV and eating. Her work suffered. Her self-esteem suffered. Her body suffered. Finally, she was persuaded by a girlfriend to come to one of my seminars on relationships, where, after listening for a while, she bravely came onstage and begged me to help her.

Leslie is typical of many of the women I see, whose pride and independence achieve much in the business arena but little in the world of love. Like Leslie, these women think of themselves as female but, inadvertently and unconsciously, take the male, pursuer role in a relationship.

Unfortunately, so many women are acting aggressively toward men that it is assumed to be correct behavior. But aggressive behavior is correct *only* in certain situations. Leslie needed to learn about her choices—male, female; pursuer, pursued; giver, receiver—and understand that she unconsciously took the male, pursuer, giver role. When a woman like Leslie pretends to be the sexually generous male partner even though she really wants to receive lovemaking in a committed relationship as the female partner, she ends up frustrated and confused.

My plan was to instruct Leslie about the options, choices, and techniques she needed to achieve her goal of a serious relationship. I was to act somewhat like a parent in an age when most parents are bewildered when it comes to teaching mating practices.

I asked Leslie to let me be her coach until she found her man. She started to cry, not really daring to believe that I could help her. However, I have seen enough success stories to be able to promise fulfillment, and I did so with Leslie.

When Leslie asked at what point I thought her relationship with Mark had begun to go wrong, I replied, "The first moment, when by pursuing Mark, you unknowingly chose to be the male in your relationship. He who speaks first is male. If you had chosen to be female, you would have flirted with your eyes and your smile and let him pursue you."

Leslie picked sexy men, whom she approached first. In this way, she unconsciously and automatically set up the relationship so that she would never get to be the sexy, cherished woman. If Leslie really wanted to be pursued and loved by a generous, protective, and cherishing man, she would have to learn to be passively potent and magnetic.

Leslie believed that by giving her body to Mark, she would make him fall in love with her and later make a commitment to her. But handsome and successful men like Mark have been trained out of their generous, protective, and cherishing mating skills by women like Leslie who do all the work. Once Leslie had sex with Mark without requiring a commitment first, he had no reason to cherish her feelings or reward her with love and commitment. He saw and respected her as an independent woman. He accepted her generous, sensuous, sexual gifts without any guilt, shame, or need to commit, because he believed that she had thought out her desire for physical, social, and sexual pleasure and knew how to avoid painful situations. In other words, by earning respect for giving, Leslie lost the right to be cherished by Mark as a vulnerable woman.

Both Leslie and Mark believed that traditionalism in roles was a thing of the past. Neither saw their parents' marriage as one they would wish for, but "low-maintenance" women like Leslie are giving more and getting less than their mothers did before the women's movement. Neither Leslie nor Mark realized that their mothers were not just "giving." They were, in fact, *giving back*, to men who had been committed enough to marry them and to be respectable and responsible for their welfare. But Leslie was giving Mark all the benefits of a wife without requiring a commitment from him.

If Leslie had loved herself more than she loved Mark, she would have required a committed relationship. If he didn't agree to a commitment, she could say "No, thank you" without fear of loss. Better to lose him than herself. Instead, Leslie gave Mark sex at no cost of commitment, which ultimately led to her becoming used by him. He took all she would give until she sent him a bill of guilt, which caused him to leave for a better deal.

Leslie and Mark believed in equality, which to them meant that both could have their thinking respected and their feelings cherished by the other, equally. Unfortunately, in a love affair duplication equals competition. Their equality blew up the night Leslie learned that her friend had died and Mark had a business problem. Both needed help. Both wanted to be given to, Leslie emotionally and Mark logically. The collision resulted in the beginning of the end of their relationship. Since they had not negotiated respect and cherishing priorities before entering the sexual area, neither felt cherished or respected.

If they had negotiated, and Mark had chosen to be the "male" energy and Leslie the "female," he would have known that by giving Leslie some emotional loving support on the night her friend died, he would have been given back all the logical help a comfortable woman can give.

When the relationship came apart, Leslie immediately went into a doormat mode: "I need him at any cost; I'll do what he wants." Her response was to give more, rather than to evaluate what she had not received in the way of compassion.

Seeing Leslie totally neglect her own needs in favor of his

elicited dark disgust in Mark's nature. It was as if she invited abuse. He unconsciously became cold and punitive, thus getting more out of Leslie in her panic. He was totally into control and Leslie totally out of control, and she reached rock bottom on the evening she drove her car off violently. When verbal communication fails, violence ensues.

Leslie began coming regularly to my seminars, persisting in her quest for a loving relationship that would endure. She began to "duty-date" (my way of describing that tedious, boring process of exposing oneself to people one really doesn't feel attracted to, until one finds someone one *does* feel attracted to), wherein she was the bait, not the masculine pursuer.

At first, being a magnetic, sexual, sensuous woman made Leslie feel vulnerable and a little frightened. She was used to being in control. But I taught her that being vulnerable *was* safe, as long as she didn't allow dangerous things to take place, for example, going home with a man she didn't know and having casual sex with him. She had to learn how to control herself without trying to control the man she was with.

Leslie shared her stories about her romantic life in my seminars and asked questions about how to deal with each situation. She found that she did well with duty dates, but when she was with men she liked, she inevitably went back to her old ways, only to end up with a broken heart.

Then, one evening she came up onstage and told us about Walt, a free-lance photographer she'd met through business.

Their first date was a picnic on the beach. They had a great time, easily touching and affectionately kissing. She learned that although Walt did not have much financial stability, he was fun, easygoing, and spontaneous. Playing with Walt allowed her to *feel* feminine, sensual, sexual, and physical. She liked him a lot, although she couldn't help wishing he had a stronger, more assured financial future.

Leslie dated Walt regularly but nonsexually for more than two months, at which time he asked Leslie for a commitment. When she mentioned her financial concerns, he explained that when they married and had children, he would climb the corporate ladder. He would do it for his family, but not for himself alone. He needed inspiration.

He told her that he would like her to continue working full-time until the first baby was born. Then he wanted her to consider either just working part-time or staying at home with their child.

Leslie thought over Walt's proposal and accepted. Soon after their marriage, Walt got a terrific job on a magazine, and money started rolling in just as he said it would. After Leslie gave birth to their son, she worked for a little while but then quit. She and Walt have plans to gradually build his home studio into their business together.

Although Leslie had started out as a career woman, she was now a woman with a career on the side. Some women want to be career women, but not Leslie.

ANDREA

Andrea, a real estate broker, wondered what was wrong with her. Why couldn't she make a relationship work? Why did every man she met seem to compete with her? Her sister, Margaret, who was not as pretty or smart as she was, had married two years earlier and was expecting her first child. Andrea just couldn't figure it out.

Then one of her customers brought her to my seminar. After hearing me speak, Andrea concluded that she had been too "masculine" in her past relationships with men and vowed that she would now change, using my step-by-step method for the "feminine" woman she was determined to be.

She met Johnny, an insurance salesman, through a friend. He asked her out almost immediately. One delightful date followed another, and their relationship took off into one of commitment and planning for the future.

At first, Andrea followed my "rules of femininity" as carefully as she could. She listened to Johnny's ideas and thoughts, responded with her feelings, and enlisted his opinions on things before voicing her own. She didn't tell him what to do, she didn't call him, and she didn't plan their social life—all things she had done with men in the past.

But somewhere around the fourth month, Andrea's natural self began to emerge, when she began instigating the social events in their lives, being careful they fit in with her work schedule rather than his. She also started giving Johnny gifts, first a VCR and then various items of clothes. Soon, whenever Johnny tried to convince Andrea about some idea he had, instead of just telling her "feelings," she began to respond with her own enthusiastic ideas. In fact, in no time she was telling Johnny her opinions about everything, including the various ways she thought he could improve.

The more she began to assert herself, the more he began to pull away. He saw her enthusiastic ideas as either implementing or supplementing his own. Before long, Johnny was snapping and Andrea was attacking, because she felt that he did not listen to or respect her opinions. Little by little, without Andrea understanding why, the warmth and promise of the relationship was going. Johnny felt himself slipping into frustration, into what seemed to him like a secondary position, and soon began an affair with a young assistant at his office.

When Andrea discovered the affair, she ended their relationship, but she was in pain, confused over why Johnny could reject her in favor of the other woman. She felt bewildered, but after listening to her story, I suggested that she might be following the wrong principles. I believed that she was a woman driven by a masculine type of energy.

I explained that her training from her mother *and* father, by the type of woman he had chosen, was to be a feminine-energized, receptive, cherished woman. However, her own nature was to be an assertive, respected, career-oriented woman, meaning a woman with a masculine-energy approach rather than the feminine-energy approach that her mother and sister employed. Andrea had initially been doing what she thought was the correct, socially accepted technique but found her real self surfacing after the relationship was established.

By suppressing her inherent inclinations, she was creating a powder keg that would unavoidably explode. The trick was to discover herself, not remake herself.

I suggested that she now go out into the dating market with a different approach, and that she begin to express her thoughts and wants freely.

"If you find someone you like," I said, "tell him you would like to go out with him. When you come on with a receptive, feminine-type demeanor, you're attracting the wrong men for you, because you're attracting men who want to lead, instigate, and give first. But that is exactly what you really want to do, so you must find the opposite in a man."

A quick-change attitude wasn't easy for Andrea, since she had watched her mother and sister deal with men in the traditional way and had been taught that this was the only acceptable way for a lady to act to attract a man. But with my encouragement, she determined to give the other approach a try. A few weeks later, Andrea attended a singles' party; she met three men and asked each for their card. Later in the week she called them, talked briefly and cordially to each, then suggested the two of them get together for a drink. One of the men rejected her offer, and two accepted.

Daniel, an accountant, the first man she met for a drink, clearly hoped that Andrea would be a fast-and-free playmate. He was turned off when he discovered that her assertive approach did not mean she wanted casual sex. Andrea was looking for a committed relationship with the right man, not a wild and sexual fling. Their second meeting was their last. Andrea knew he was not for her.

Ryan, the second man, accepted Andrea's invitation to have dinner. He was an artist who was fascinated by Andrea's business prowess and her intelligence. Andrea relaxed into the relationship from the onset, giving to Ryan first and cherishing his feelings.

This was a perfect relationship for Ryan, who got no thrill out of aggressively competing in the world of business. He was delighted when Andrea suggested that she organize a showing of his paintings at a friend's gallery, thereby promoting his work. Ryan was comfortable with her energy and takeover disposition, which was a wonderful complement to his own more introspective and artistic inclinations.

They married at the end of their first year together, and when their first son was born, Andrea stayed home with him for the first six months, then went back full-time to work. Ryan had shared in the child-caring activities from the beginning but then took over most of these since he worked in the home. Although not conventional, they are a very happy couple, and very well suited to one another.

Leslie decided to be the feminine energy in her relationship, and Andrea chose the male energy as best suited for her. Now it is your turn to make the decision. The next chapter will give you some clues about how to do it.

CHAPTER 3

Choosing to Be Respected or Cherished

Relationships often falter from the start because we enter them with confused needs and expectations. I have found that the best way for you to clarify these issues for yourself is to ask yourself the following question: Which is my greatest need—to be cherished for my feelings or respected for my thoughts?

If you want your thinking respected first, you will choose to be the "male" energy, and if you want your feelings cherished first, you will choose to be the "female" energy.

Successful relationships are an exchange of *opposite* energies, so the goal is to be able to make a clear decision about your energy system before you begin a relationship. You cannot chaotically or spontaneously jump back and forth between the two, being both actively masculine and passively feminine. That destroys relationships and wears down one or both people.

You can see how destructive it was for Leslie and Mark's relationship when she gave off confused signals by first appearing to be masculine when she approached him and had sex with him, and then switching to feminine when she wanted her feelings to be cherished.

Mark, who was not about to turn her freebies down, was quickly spoiled by Leslie, then confused by her "quick change."

He couldn't really get a footing on their relationship, and he left. He certainly didn't feel inclined to give her a commitment.

With Andrea as well, each relationship she entered was fated to end badly because the feminine energy she presented to each man initially was quickly eroded by her real masculine energy.

Neither woman, though educated, smart, and attractive, was able to walk into a relationship and have it blossom into happiness forever. So I wish to stress again that the key is to know yourself, know which energy you are comfortable with, and *ground* yourself in that choice before you enter a relationship.

Consider an aggressive, gregarious woman who knows what she likes in a man immediately and enjoys approaching him to start a relationship. If the man she approaches is predominantly female-energy based, or passive, things *could* work out. But if this man also enjoys the conquest of going after a woman and catching her, a relationship between these two people is ill-fated. Neither will feel the satisfaction of his or her basic drive to assert and initiate.

On the other hand, what about a woman who spots a man she is drawn to, but who, every time he looks her way, looks down for fear of seeming too forward. If this man is drawn to her but is too fearful of being rejected to approach her, how can they get together? Both the man and woman are passive receivers and not aggressive initiators.

Although I believe that there are only two basic games in town—involving money (male) and sex (female)—it is obvious that in this day and age, simultaneous careers of equal financial reward are common. How to make the relationship work? By making sure that the two people flow with the energy exchange and don't trample on one another.

Marcy and Burt, both computer programmers earning roughly the same salaries, met on a blind date and liked one another. The next day, each was in the other's thoughts, and both wanted to have the relationship develop. However, Marcy, who wanted to be the feminine energy, did not call Burt. She waited for him to call her. Two days later, he called to invite her out, and she said yes. This set the pattern for Burt to be the masculine and Marcy the feminine energy, even though they were basically equal in earning power.

Being equal in career and brains does not mean being equal in energy preference. Everyone has innate talents and preferences. One person likes to make reservations or pay bills, while the other likes to cook or prefers initiating sex. When a man and woman are "equal" in career and brains, they can talk about likes and preferences and personal talents that make one of them better suited for some of the various mental and physical requirements of being a couple.

When two people have parallel incomes, the delineating line is still who is the active, giving masculine energy and who is the passive, receptive feminine energy. In other words, *who is respected and who is cherished?*

HOW TO RESPECT OR CHERISH THE OTHER

If you choose to be the "female" energy, respecting your man's thinking ahead of your own means that whether the ideas, desires, or opinions that he is sharing agree or disagree with yours, you must listen, revere, honor, esteem, and accept them, or negotiate a change in such a way (which I will teach you) so that he feels respected.

If you choose to be the "male" energy, cherishing your man's feelings ahead of your own means that whether his feelings are positive or negative, you listen, accept, honor, and revere them, and then negotiate some form of joint behavioral change (which I will teach you) that will make him feel better.

Can you be the female energy, make more money than your man, and still respect him? Of course!

Jerome, an associate professor of literature, made about half as much money as his girlfriend, Suzzett, a caterer. However, Jerome was clearly the male in the relationship, and Suzzett admired and respected his position and intellect.

Suzzett, the cherished one, brought sensuality into the life of the couple. When Jerome went to Suzzett's apartment after work, he could relax there with her. She provided a comfortable and loving environment.

After nine months of being in a mutually exclusive, long-term sexual relationship, Suzzett knew she wanted to marry Jerome. She still felt that tingling feeling when he talked to her decisively and told her what he wanted, whether it was a date or making love. She needed her man to be the leader in the relationship, and when Jerome led her to where he wanted her to go, she responded sensuously and sexually, out of a feeling of security and safety, two necessary issues for her to be sexually vulnerable.

And Jerome loved her vulnerability. It was a sexual turn-on for him to feel the pleasure control in his hands. He knew she trusted him, and because she did, he could be more risk-taking and creatively confident about leading and pleasing her sexually. She brought out his masculinity sexually, and he brought out her femininity sexually. This sealed their intimacy.

For Suzzett and Jerome, the relationship was balanced. He wanted to be respected as his first priority, and she wanted to be cherished.

When both people in a relationship expect their feelings to be cherished or their ideas and logic to be respected simultaneously, a conflict in the form of a push-pull power play occurs.

To give an example, going to a movie is a simple thing to do, but when you both have different movies in mind, it could become a problem. That's what happened to Laurie, a manicurist, whenever she wanted to see a romance film, and her boyfriend, Al, a used-car salesman, wanted to see a Western.

In the past, Laurie had wanted to be with Al so much and was so afraid of losing him that she allowed him to intimidate her into seeing any movie he wanted, no matter what she really felt. But she realized she was becoming angry over the way she was handling the situation. I taught her how to talk to Al so that he could cherish her feelings and not try to intimidate her into his choice, while she respected his choice and didn't try to seduce him with her feelings.

The next time Al began to intimidate her into going with him to a Western she didn't want to see, she told him that she was willing to see it because she wanted to be with him (respecting him), but she also told him her feelings, which were that she really didn't like "shoot-'em-ups." The result was that Al heard what she said and cherished her feelings. They compromised on a third movie, one that he liked and about which she felt good.

Beware of men who will neither respect you nor cherish you, as a way to keep painful distance between you. They are afraid of intimacy. Superficiality is the goal of nonintimate people. Getting money and having sex are the goals of superficial couples. Sharing feelings and thoughts are the goals of truly loving, vulnerable men and women.

WHAT ABOUT ANATOMY? (HORMONES)

Although the social-sexual revolution freed us to be either the male or female energy in a relationship, we will examine how anatomy plays a major role in shaping our choices. We will discuss how gender contributes powerfully to our energy preferences, with most women still wanting to be the feminine energy and most men the masculine energy.

Freud said, "Anatomy is destiny," and this is true because of the hormonal balance of our bodies.

Most women I encounter (under the age of fifty) fall naturally into being the "feminine" energy. Their primary interest (even though most of them have to earn a living) is in relationships, because that is where the female hormone, *estrogen*, leads them.

Estrogen is an affect (feeling) hormone. It keeps women caring more about feelings and emotions than cars and jobs. The female principles are "I feel" and "I don't want pain." The ultimate feminine issue is making love, because it is the closest and most intimate thing that two people can do.

Because of his male hormone, *testosterone*, the man under

fifty will be driven to action (doing) and will prefer to be the male energy. According to their nature, what most men want most in life is power, money, and sex, because this is where their testosterone leads them. In the real world, this translates into most men being interested in buying, selling, and building. Their world is concrete and performance-oriented. The male principles are "I think" and "I want."

A young man who is influenced by his testosterone will want to "produce" and "perform." His masculine energy, which is selfless, likes to perform a task so that he can feel good about the product. Often he will perform for the intellectual pleasure of achieving his goal of money, power, and prestige. Of course, each of us has a time of performance, but men's bodies are built more for performance than process.

A woman who is influenced by her estrogen processes her feelings and thoughts, which keeps her in constant touch with them so she can make a decision to move toward pleasure if she "feels" good, or stop actions if she "feels" bad. Processing allows a woman to continually track her feelings and to act on them, especially avoiding painful experiences by saying no.

I often say that women need to "feel good" to do good, but men need to "do good" to feel good. For example, because of the way testosterone affects a man, he will be less likely than a woman to experience discomfort working in an unaesthetic environment. This is because he can focus on the task at hand with less sensitivity to people and things around him. What is seen as insensitivity by his woman is seen by the man as an efficient, effective, and economical system at work.

However, as time goes by, we see a reversal, when nature naturally pushes us toward our opposite role. In the second half of life, men become more passively feminine. Their testosterone lowers, making them less aggressive and more receptive. The estrogen in their system promotes sensitivity and feeling. Women, however, become more actively masculine after menopause, when their estrogen level drops and the progesterone impacts them more. Often, women then go out into the money world to make their mark while men are ready to retire to their homes and pleasures such as cooking, gardening, doing some kind of artwork, listening to music.

In her book *Second Honeymoon*, Dr. Sonya Rhodes talks of the "mid-life—role swapping" in which "men who manage mid-life well become more receptive to the 'affiliative' (the nurturing and sensual) aspects of themselves, while women who thrive in mid-life become more assertive and 'autonomous' to negotiate equitably and voluntarily, with pride and ego set aside."

By the way, since postmenopausal women are often more logical and stable than younger women, they often communicate with masculine men better than younger women. For this reason, older women and younger men often do well together. A younger man's testosterone and an older woman's progesterone allow them to be a good team and to perform well, especially in money-making endeavors. Older women in the work force are often easier for men to get along with.

THE BRAIN DIFFERENCES

Another anatomical indicator that modifies and shapes our choices is the lobes of the brain. The left lobe is the thinking, verbal, and actively "masculine" lobe, and the right one is the feeling, nonverbal, receptively "feminine" lobe. Between these is a fibrous mass called the corpus callosum that processes information from both lobes. Because this transmitting tissue is smaller in right-handed men than it is in left-handed men or in women, generally right-handed men act from either their left lobe (teaching, verbalizing, problem-solving, solution-giving) *or* their right lobe (sensuous, nonverbal, sexual), but rarely from both right and left lobes at the same time.

However, a woman, because her corpus callosum is larger, *is* capable of processing data both from her right and left lobes at the same time, in effect melding her thoughts and feelings. This can cause problems in a relationship between a woman and a right-handed man, when she expects him to be able to speak freely about feelings and he expects her to be logical.

Often, a right-handed man is confused about his bright, sensitive woman, and says, "How can anyone be so smart and so dumb at the same time?"

When Terry, a policeman, surprised his wife, Lilly, a bookkeeper, by taking her to a small airfield for a jaunt in a twin-engine plane, he was irritated and amazed by her terrified reaction.

How could Lilly be so illogical? he wondered. A twin-engine was a lot safer than a jumbo jet. At least if anything went wrong, there was a chance of gliding the plane to the ground. How could Lilly handle her job if she was so illogical and emotional about this issue of flying? He couldn't help putting her down.

But Lilly wanted Terry's empathy and understanding that this was a problem for her, logical or not. She did not want his ridicule.

Collisions between Terry's logical and Lilly's "illogical" reactions had been a chronic problem between them until they heard me speak on neurological differences between women and right-handed men.

By realizing that there was actually a biological difference in their brains, Terry was able to empathize with Lilly's feelings and give her cherishing comfort, which eventually helped her desensitize her fears.

It is important to understand that empathy in itself can have a healing effect on the other person. Expressing empathy offers support while your partner works out her or his inner conflicts.

By the way, left-handed men are different from right-handed men because, like all women (both left- and right-handed), they can think *and* feel at the same time. This means they are able to speak logically, and with feelings. This can be terrific for a woman, because talking to one of these men can be like talking to your best friend. However, sometimes all hell can break loose because you both have a lot of emotion behind your thoughts and don't want to compromise.

If you and your left-handed man both have had a difficult day at work and both feel distraught and maybe a little depressed when you get together at night, you could find that because your needs for comfort are so acute, neither of you will be able to console the other. This could easily result in resentment, anger, verbal attacks, or a withdrawal of affection.

Therefore, if you are with a left-handed man, it is important that you and he make a decisive commitment early in the relationship to choose which one of you will be respected for logic and which will be cherished for his or her feelings. You must override your natural ability to think and feel at the same time.

I want to make a distinction between actions that are influenced by a physical reality, as with hormones and anatomy, and actions that are a result of a psychological dysfunction, as with Leslie and Mark when a stalemate occurred because both wanted their feelings cherished at the same time. A constant collision, male versus male, and female versus female, will undermine the natural flow of intimacy. A death grip can ensue, which can end in violence or the end of the relationship.

LANGUAGE

Your energy preference will most likely manifest itself through your language choices. If you find yourself starting sentences with "I want," and "I think," you probably want to be the "male" in the relationship. If you begin your sentences with "I don't want," and "I feel," you'll probably opt for "female."

When you choose to be the masculine energy, you do so because you want to give, protect, and cherish your intimate partner. After you say, "I think" and "I want," you must ask, "How do you feel about what I have just said?" Listening to and cherishing the feelings of your feminine-energy partner, especially her negative feelings, is the sign of a balanced masculine energy.

Practically speaking, what this means is that people who are primarily masculine energy will say things like, "I think we should do this," "I want you to love me," "I want to be with you," "I want to have sex with you. How do you feel about that?" and the female energy will say, "I feel good about that," or "I don't want to do that," or "This would make me happy, sad, glad, excited, angry."

A masculine-energy person will say, "I *want* to go to Alaska for our vacation. I *think* that will be a great place. How do you feel about that?"

The feminine-energy person will respond, "That would make me very happy. What a great idea." Or, "That doesn't make me very happy. I *don't want* to go so far away. I'd really *feel* better about someplace closer. What do you think about that?"

If you choose to be the feminine energy, do not ask your masculine man for better or more love, time, affection, or sex. You may ask for all the *things* you want, like diamonds, houses, and cars, because masculine men like giving *things*. But in the area of love, time, affection, and sex you must wait patiently for the best offer to say yes or no to. If you become impatient and go into the masculine principle, you are asking your man to be your female or your little boy, and undoubtedly he will resent it. Because he won't want to fight with you, he will go passive-aggressive instead. He will say yes to your request and then give you less than you would have gotten had you said nothing. I suggest that if a man does not meet your requirements in the area of love, affection, time, and sex, reject him and find another man.

Barney and Priscilla had been in a relationship for eight months. Barney loved her, and until recently he felt respected and she felt cherished. But lately, Barney had been working more than usual, and sometimes he wanted to cut their dates short so he could go home alone and sleep. Priscilla felt deprived of love, affection, time, and sex and decided to ask for those things. She complained, "Why can't you come over here and sleep so we can have sex? If you wanted to be with me, you would, even if you're a little tired."

Barney didn't want to argue, so he said yes to sleeping at her apartment. But instead of having sex, when he got there, he promptly fell asleep on the sofa. He was being passive-aggressive, and she was angrier than before she asked.

As time passed and Priscilla continued to nag, Barney became more distant. Priscilla got frightened. Why was he distant? Didn't he love and want her anymore? Was there someone else? Priscilla talked with a girlfriend who knew my principles and decided to come to my seminars, where she came onstage to ask for my advice.

I told her that she must either accept the situation or reject it temporarily or permanently. Women do not have *nagging* rights, only *leaving* rights. She learned to ground herself in her feminine energy and approach Barney with *validation.*

"Barney," she said, "I sense [believe, feel] that something is wrong. You seem angry [tired, bored, distant]. You haven't touched me the way you used to, and you don't make love to me very often now. Am I right?"

Barney appreciated what she said and told her there was no one else he wanted. He reiterated that he just needed his sleep. Priscilla stopped nagging, and when Barney's overtime work schedule ended, he treated her with more love and affection; they had more sex and time together than ever. He appreciated her accepting him as he was and trusting him.

IT'S YOUR CHOICE

In these days of sensitive men and powerful women, not all men *want* to be the "male" and carry the responsibility of caring for others, nor do all women want to give up their independent rights and be the "female." That is fine. We are all born with our physical capabilities, our mental intelligence and temperament. We have the freedom and ability to choose whether we want to be the masculine or feminine energy, and while hormones, brain differences, language patterns, and styles may direct us toward certain choices, we must finally be guided by what feels most natural to us.

The women's movement has begun to free women's masculine energy at work and in relationships. Now, the men's movement, personified by Robert Bly in his book *Iron John*, asks women to allow men to experience and express their masculine "red Knight, wild man" shark energy before being pressured to prematurely suppress it and become "white Knights."

If men are allowed to integrate their feminine (anima) in their own time frame, not in a woman's, it will be more an authentic, loving, and sensitive experience, and less a "good boy" passive-aggressive one.

Women who try to control men out of fear of their own vulnerability in masculine potency attempt to castrate the "red Knight," but end up paying for it as men learn to hate women's castrating power.

However, the men's movement has also begun to free men's feminine energy without their feeling guilty. Many of these men feel more authentic in roles formerly allocated to women: homemaker, primary caretaker of children, monitor of the family's social calendar.

Feminine-energy men do not like to fight, but they do appreciate masculine women who like to compete, lead, and often be the major provider of status and money and generally take charge outside the relationship. Within the relationship, feminine men feel respected when their feelings are cherished, and masculine women feel cherished when their ideas are respected. They complement each other's needs.

Feminine men are not repressed homosexuals or pathological, weird, wimpy, or weak. Often a dynamic, masculine-energy woman will see a gentle and sensitive man as weak, until he leaves her because she did not respect him.

Usually, it is the masculine-energy partner who brings status and security to the relationship. But often, feminine-energy men use their sensitivity, creativity, and intuition to make a lot of money. They often own the best art galleries, hotels, and restaurants. As individual career professionals, they make the best doctors, writers, actors, artists, and teachers. Their feminine energy along with their material physical maleness lends itself to good human loving interaction, and thus good business follows. But whatever his profession, the feminine-energy man will basically be a sensitive man who can offer sensuality and sexuality to a strong woman who will back up his career with her brains. In a world where men *should* be men and women *should* be women, these alternative lifestyle couples need to read and hear that they are normal and healthy.

Henry, a brilliant, sensitive, somewhat shy internist who was uncomfortable pursuing women, met Cynthia, an intelligent, strong, and attractive nurse, in the hospital he was affiliated with. Cynthia easily initiated their dating relationship, they made a commitment to one another, and a year later they married.

During the first few years of their marriage, Cynthia ran Henry's office. The combination of Cynthia's organizational skills and Henry's great bedside manner proved powerful, and Henry became very successful.

When the children began arriving, she quit working at the office but never abandoned him for the kids, or his practice, which she controlled from home. When they were at home together, she backed off driving him as a doctor and cherished his need to relax and play Dad with their three kids. She saw to it that he did not have to worry about bills being paid or their house being remodeled. She handled it all, quietly and efficiently.

Some feminine-energy men will not have a career. They function best in areas where relationships are important, such as home, children, and romance. Some women don't enjoy these areas but do want a home and family and are willing to become career women to bring home the money and status to provide a nice life for the family. Each of us must look inside ourselves, examine our real desires, and then act on them.

Many wonderful men who choose to be the feminine energy in a relationship are out there, and they are the complementary romantic choice to seek if you happen to be the type of woman who wants to be respected in your relationship. If you are this kind of woman, you like being in control and having a loving man share your life. It's part of your nature. You like giving;

you like protecting; you like cherishing. Respecting and accepting men's choices of using their creativity aesthetically in the home and sensitivity in their relationships is the only logical balance to the masculine-energy woman.

The main question you must ask yourself is, "Am I a woman with a career or a career woman?" If you see yourself as a woman with a career, you probably have to make some professional sacrifices in that career to enhance your man's career prospects, such as giving up a great job position and moving to another city because his promotion includes a relocation, or even giving up your career while you are raising the children and then, perhaps, resuming the career later.

If you are a career woman and refuse to compromise on building your empire, you should be looking for a feminine-energy male who will help run the home as well as support your career needs without resentments.

Glen, a successful owner of a small franchise printing shop, liked the goals of his girlfriend, Antoinette. She had begun a small children's clothing boutique in her home and was now a manufacturer with her own label.

As she became more successful, Antoinette was less available to Glen and often broke dates with him because of her many meetings, travel, and hours on the phone. But Glen didn't mind. He quietly went about his own life, entertaining himself. When Antoinette was happy with her career, she was fun to play with, and that's what Glen wanted. He was willing to receive what time and energy she had to give him. He loved her for herself, not what she could or would do for him.

Glen never doubted himself when friends would tease him about being a "wimp." He and Antoinette fit together in their own way, and it didn't matter to him what others thought.

There is a time to put career ahead of womanhood, and there is a time for womanhood ahead of career. The biggest mistake is trying to do both at the same time. I usually recommend that young women get ready for a big career after the age of forty-five but prepare for womanhood early. Ask yourself, "What is my priority today? Career or family?" Once you have decided, act accordingly and find the man who supports either priority.

I am often asked whether a masculine woman can choose to become feminine, and whether a career woman can change and become a woman with a career. The answer is yes, but if she does decide to change, she has to be able to receive a man's masculine leadership without rebelling against him, which isn't easy for a woman who has been living in the masculine energy.

If this is you, please evaluate your *real* desires about being the strong leader or the feminine follower *before* you begin a relationship, not afterward. Otherwise, you will find yourself fighting your man for the throne.

Performance and productivity are masculine, whether at work or at home. If you choose to be a woman with a career on the side, you must "follow" your "leader" husband in all areas of marriage, including child raising, home decorating, finance, and so on.

Although you have the "feeling" veto, you are not "the boss." If you pretend that you like being the "little woman" when you really want to "run the show," you will confuse both of you, become resentful, and spend your productive energy trying to control him and undermine his self-esteem. So make an authentic choice of career woman or woman with a career.

It is better to have a powerful woman in a relationship with a sensitive, loving man than to have a woman acting helpless with a sensitive man, trying to build up his image, when he's not going to change. This is because when she finally reveals herself fully, and she will, she will cut him down instead of cherishing him, and she will rob him of his male potency. She will resent him for not being the masculine energy to her feminine-energy pretense, at which time the relationship will come to an end.

Remember, pretense has no place in relationships. Be grounded in self-awareness, confidence, and integrity.

CHAPTER 4

Is Giving Masculine or Feminine?

L ike Leslie, many women have been trained, in some cases by their feminine fathers who wanted them to be another "Mommy," that giving is a feminine skill, and receiving is the right and privilege of the "real" man. These women feel they have to get out there and do something in order for a man to love them.

It frustrates me when a young man comes into my office complaining, "I take her out on one date, and she calls me for three. I buy her one dinner, and she has me over for four dinners. I send her a card, she sends me a fabulous gift." Then his girlfriend comes into my office and says, "I treat him so well; why won't he give me a commitment?"

In a rational family, a woman is taught to love herself first. If, however, she is raised in a family where her father wanted his feelings taken care of before his wife's or his daughter's (and did not give back lovingly), she cannot develop self-love. An example of this kind of man would be an alcoholic, a workaholic, a violent or abusive man, or one who expressed high-performance expectations of his daughter.

Let me make the distinction between the healthy identification of a girl with her father, as with Andrea, and a young woman who is not cherished by her father but is only validated by him if she performs. This kind of woman will usually be a mother to the men in her life.

When they are under the age of five, a healthy mother loves

her children better than herself. However, when the children get older, she'd better start switching back to being self-centered.

If you look back at your own childhood, and your mother was giving, protecting, and cherishing her family, you're seeing someone who forgot to go back to her *womanhood* after she had her babies. Mothering is a terminal illness when used on able-bodied people over the age of five, who can do for themselves. Women who mother their husbands eventually either drive them away or subdue them until they cannot stand alone.

Unfortunately, many women never get over an attack of motherhood. One of my male clients told me that his wife changed into a mother when she gave birth and remained primarily a mother. That man lost his woman to his son. And that is unhealthy. Any parent who puts the child ahead of his or her mate is not married in the real sense, in my opinion. That person can be legally bound, but not intimately married.

When a woman is selfless with a son over five, she is doing *him* a great disservice, because he will have the impression that all women should be "givers." This will cause problems in his relationships with women, and he can easily become the kind of man Dan Kiley talks about in his book *The Peter Pan Syndrome*. These are narcissistic "little boys" who have not grown into healthy manhood. They do not have the ability to love, protect, cherish, give back, or assume responsibility.

A "Peter Pan"–type man expects his woman to take better care of him than of herself. He will get her to make the dinner or theater reservations, lend him money, pick him up for a date, or pick out his mother's birthday present because he's too busy to do it himself.

Unless you want to be his "mother," you must learn to say no to these requests. The feminine energy is not giving, because giving is action, and femininity, whether in women or men, is passivity. For a true balance of energy, women must give back to men who graciously give, protect, and cherish them first.

When a man can give, protect, and cherish his woman above himself, he has matured to "selflessness" and he will be rewarded by those he loves. But if instead of giving, protecting, and cherishing his woman above himself, he says, "That's not fair. Why do I have to give first? Why doesn't she give first? My mom gave to my dad, and they've been married thirty-five years," my answer is "Your mom was selfless, therefore masculine, and your dad was feminine or a 'Peter Pan,' depending on whether he was able to give back or not."

A masculine-energy man *does not* marry a woman who gives to him, unless he is a "little boy" who wants to be mothered. A masculine man marries a feminine woman who is available to receive from him, who respects him for giving, and who knows how to give back to reward him but always a little less than she gets. That might mean cooking a nice meal, occasionally taking him to a movie or the theater, or giving him a little gift or card that he might like. The only stipulation is that she *not* give back *more* than he has given her, which would put him in the feminine, receiver position and perhaps make him feel smothered as well.

If you are a healthy, feminine woman, you are self-centered. You love yourself first, before any man. Then you share that love with your man and your loved ones. You say no to people, places, and things that hurt you in any way. You say no to whatever strikes you as unethical. You say no to the man you love. You say, "I don't feel good about doing what you ask, and I will not do it without retribution, even if it causes you pain. I would rather cause you pain by saying *no* than hurt myself by saying yes." Sometimes you must also be able to say, "I'm not going to put up with what you do. I'm going to leave you now."

When you say no to what you don't want, you are faced with two responses from a man. Either he'll say, "You deserve someone better than me. I don't have what you need or want," or he will say, "I will find the things you want by experimenting and creating. I will find out what turns you on."

If you know what you don't want from him, he will figure out what you do want, by investing time, money, and energy. It is good for him to solve the problem, and he will feel good about himself when he is appreciated as giving, protective, and cherishing.

Masculine men like problems and challenges. They like the chase. "Little boys" like Mama to do it for them; they don't want you to ask them for anything at all. Women who attempt to control seductively by saying yes to everything and suppressing feelings are insecure and inadequate as women.

A masculine man is turned off by a yes-woman, because he knows she is needy, dependent, guilt-inducing, and easily manipulated by *any* man. He needs to trust your no to believe your yes. He has to be able to trust your virtue after marriage. Men know other men. They know that men go after what they want (the woman) and will get her, unless she loves herself better than she loves a man. However, a man must love his woman better than himself, or he will use and abuse her if she allows it. If you can learn to say no, you will have the satisfaction of knowing that you can never be used by a man. A man can "propose" anything, but you must say yes or no to remain emotionally balanced and in control.

So remember, if it doesn't feel good, don't do it, no matter who is demanding. The casting couch, the boardroom couch, the marriage bed, the cash register, the baby bassinet—all invite a confused woman to sell out her total balanced life, which should be designed by herself for herself and no others.

If, however, a woman chooses to be the masculine energy, to be selfless and love others ahead of herself, and she is comfortable doing so, she will thrive. Masculine men *like* being needed, but feminine men do not. They are more comfortable with a woman who likes to take responsibility, leaving him to be the more artistic, fun element in the relationship.

Both styles are appropriate for their complementary woman—a masculine-energy man with a feminine-energy, receiving woman, and a feminine-energy man with a giving, masculine-energy woman. One selfless giver and one self-centered receiver make a perfect loop and a fertile medium for sex and romance.

Fran, the manager of a beauty supply house, and Jack, who worked in an art gallery, met at a coffeehouse, liked each other, and exchanged cards. As often happens, they intuitively sensed each other's sensitivity and found it magnetic. Jack generally felt more comfortable when the woman he was interested in took the risk to signal him that he was wanted. Fran felt the same way about men. Both put a priority on magnetic feminine energy rather than dynamic masculine energy. Before their relationship could move forward, one of them had to decide to be masculine and speak up, asking for a date of some type.

In this case, neither of them made the move, and the exchanged cards only reminded each of a lost chance.

Dotty, a secretary, and Thomas, a policeman, also failed to have a relationship, because both wanted to be in charge. They met through a dating service and had a good time on their first date. Although Thomas made it clear that he liked to be in control of a relationship and would be in touch with her, Dotty couldn't wait and called him a few days later, much to his annoyance. In fact, he asked her not to call again, and he never again called her. Dotty had to learn that she must either find a feminine man who likes being chased, or be a feminine woman who will wait to be chased.

In my seminar, Dotty learned that she really preferred being the more passive, feminine energy. At the same seminar, Arnold, an aspiring television writer, decided that he preferred to be the masculine leader with a feminine woman.

They met one evening at the social hour I hold after each seminar. Dotty liked Arnold, smiled at him, and waited for him to approach her. He did approach and began talking, then asked her for a date, which she accepted.

When Arnold began courting her by taking her out and buying her presents, Dotty managed always to give back less, which made Arnold feel good. They were opposites in energy and complemented each other enough to function without many collisions or power plays.

If you are a giving, masculine-energy woman who wants to go feminine, *stop giving* and sit passively until "he" gets the message and talks to you about negotiating a more balanced deal. *Don't give advice*, since that is more giving.

A few months ago, a woman named June, the beautiful owner of a talent agency, came to my women's group to deal with her boyfriend of two years, Sam. He insisted she do all the long-distance driving from her house in L.A. to his house in Long Beach, where he constantly invited other people to join them on their dates as a way of blocking intimacy. He refused to consider marriage. June had agreed to his terms. Lacking a strong sense of self-esteem, she feared that if she left Sam, no one else would want her.

After a few group sessions, however, June decided, although reluctantly, to put her foot down and to stop driving to see Sam. Shakily, she told him so. He immediately began driving to see her. June found that the less she gave to Sam, the more he gave to her, and as a result June began to feel more desirable and saw Sam as less so. In fact, she began to see him in a different light. He seemed superficial and shallow, and now, because she was more confident and grounded in her self-love, she realized that this was not the kind of man she wanted to invest her life in.

She made a very strong decision and broke off the relationship. Now, instead of calling Sam, she called group members when the urge to see him arose, and "duty-dated" to distract herself while waiting for a man who could offer her a better deal.

What does all this mean in terms of the stereotypical image of the self-sacrificing woman? It means that image is *wrong*. This image is exactly the one that the women's movement is confronting, often to the point of going to the extreme polarity. Sometimes women are advocating not only "Don't give," but "Don't even give back," or "Just be yourself, you don't need him, and you don't need to compromise for him." But somewhere between demanding individual rights and melding into a relationship lies my premise of "giving" and "giving back."

If you choose to be the feminine energy in a relationship, please take this pledge:

"I PROMISE NEVER TO GIVE ANYTHING TO A MAN UNLESS HE IS UNDER FIVE YEARS OF AGE OR SICK IN BED, UNLESS THERE'S SOMETHING IN IT FOR ME FIRST."

CHAPTER 5

Are You the Woman You Think You Are?

QUIZ

Check the letter, (a), (b), or (c), that most reflects the way you would behave in the situation. (Your answers are evaluated at the end of the question section.)

1. You enjoy living alone because
   (a) You don't have to deal with other people.
   (b) You have more time to work.
   (c) You enjoy the time it affords you after work, to please yourself.

2. You and your fiancé are buying a house. You have more money to invest than he does. What do you do?
   (a) Put in more money.
   (b) Put in your half share only.
   (c) Expect him to provide a house for you.

3. You enjoy working more than playing because
   (a) Playing is "feeling-centered" and you do not want to waste time.
   (b) Work produces money with which you can exert influence and greater control.
   (c) Your father expected performance from you and rewarded you with love.

4. Your boyfriend likes to camp out, and you don't. What do you do?
   (a) Go along and be a good sport.
   (b) Stay home because you do not want to go.
   (c) Insist he give up his hobby.

5. You like to masturbate, but your boyfriend feels insulted. What do you do?
   - (a) Maintain your right to please yourself when alone.
   - (b) Call him up when you want sex.
   - (c) Lie to him and allow both styles of sexual pleasure.

6. You and your boyfriend are saving for a summer rental, and he wants to control your money. What do you do?
   - (a) Refuse to do it.
   - (b) Do it with a guaranteed allowance.
   - (c) Demand that you alternate control monthly.

7. Your car has broken down. What do you do?
   - (a) Call your boyfriend and ask him to come get you.
   - (b) Leave the car and take a bus or cab home.
   - (c) Call your brother instead of your boyfriend.

8. You are in a relationship with an up-and-coming man and want to develop your own career, but he wants you to marry him and raise the kids. What do you do?
   - (a) Leave him and go off to pursue your career.
   - (b) Accept his direction as being best for your marriage.
   - (c) Say yes, and after you marry go back to your career priority.

9. You have a boyfriend who is more powerful and successful than you are. What do you do?
   - (a) "Duke it out" with him for equality.
   - (b) Surrender to his leadership and fight only over ethical and moral issues.
   - (c) Keep him awhile to see if he will surrender to you, and if not, dump him.

10. You have a fight with your gentle, feminine boyfriend, who then has a problem with impotence. What do you do?
    - (a) Accept him as he is and help him to feel safer and more relaxed.
    - (b) End the relationship and go on to the next man.
    - (c) Try to teach him with books and articles how to do it.

11. You are engaged and in a dual-career relationship, but your live-in fiancé expects you to do most of the housework, as his mom did. What do you do?
    (a) Do it to prove you are better than Mom.
    (b) Refuse to do more at home than he does, and fight with him about it.
    (c) Negotiate a fair split of chores, or leave him until he is willing.

12. Your boyfriend earns twice as much as you do but expects you to share 50-50 on dates. What do you do?
    (a) Accept this 50-50 deal for all dates.
    (b) Expect him to pay for everything.
    (c) Compromise by each paying for dates you request of the other.

13. You have a boyfriend, and you travel a great deal for your work. What do you do?
    (a) Enjoy socializing nonsexually with men out of town with your boyfriend's acceptance.
    (b) Do not socialize with men out of town because you are considerate of your boyfriend's possible hurt feelings.
    (c) Socialize secretly with men out of town.

14. Your boyfriend has been passed over for a promotion at his company. You have been invited to a company social event. What do you do?
    (a) You go to the event, but you are so angry that after a few drinks, you confront the company executive about the wrong done.
    (b) You refuse to go to the event out of anger, even though it will reflect negatively on him.
    (c) You go to the event and act like a supportive woman.

15. Both you and your boyfriend work long hours during the week and have little time for sex. What do you do?
    (a) Let him decide when to ask and say "No thank you" if you are too tired.
    (b) Initiate it when you are feeling amorous.
    (c) Negotiate to have sex only on weekends.

ANSWERS

1. You enjoy living alone because
    (a) Narcissistic
    (b) Male
    (c) Female
    Living alone to please yourself, and not to work more or avoid people, is self-loving, therefore, feminine.

2. You and your fiancé are buying a house. You have more money to invest than he does. What do you do?
    (a) Male
    (b) Female
    (c) Narcissistic
    Unless she wants to be masculine and respected, it is difficult for a feminine woman to respect and be sexual with a man when she contributes more money than he does. On the other hand, being a "gold digger" is selfish and unfeminine.

3. You enjoy working more than playing because
    (a) Male
    (b) Narcissistic
    (c) Female
    Feelings don't count. Money does. Controlling your life is more important than having fun. If Dad wanted you to perform for his love, you will see performance as normal.

4. Your boyfriend likes to camp out, and you don't. What do you do?
    (a) Male
    (b) Female
    (c) Narcissistic
    Being able to say, "No thank you, I don't feel good about camping out," sets feminine boundaries for yourself without trying to control him with seductive generosity or intimidating demands.

5. You like to masturbate, but your boyfriend feels insulted. What do you do?
    (a) Female
    (b) Male
    (c) Narcissistic

Your body belongs to you first, therefore you have a moral right to please it. A man oversteps his bounds when he sets moral or ethical standards for you.

6. You and your boyfriend are saving for a summer rental, and he wants to control your money. What do you do?
   (a) Male
   (b) Female
   (c) Narcissistic

To respect your masculine man financially while requiring him to cherish your feelings by giving you an allowance can be an efficient way to handle money. Taking control makes you the masculine one.

7. Your car has broken down. What do you do?
   (a) Female
   (b) Male
   (c) Narcissistic

Reaching out first to your man rather than a relative honors him with respect and allows him to show you how much he cherishes you.

8. You are in a relationship with an up-and-coming man and want to develop your own career, but he wants you to marry him and raise the kids. What do you do?
   (a) Male
   (b) Female
   (c) Narcissistic

If you are a woman first and your career is second, follow him. If you are a career woman first, put your career first, but then find a feminine man who is willing to be a Mr. Mom. Or stay single.

9. You have a boyfriend who is more powerful and successful than you are. What do you do?
   (a) Male
   (b) Female
   (c) Narcissistic

Intimacy requires compromise. Competing for "equality" is normal for singles but destructive in a relationship. Equitable exchanges enhance compatibility.

10. You have a gentle, feminine boyfriend, who then has a problem with impotence. What do you do?
    (a) Female
    (b) Male
    (c) Narcissistic
    A man's penis cannot be "taught." Create a safe harbor without giving instructions and make your body available. Nature will take its course, and you will either become lovers or end up as friends.

11. You are engaged and in a dual-career relationship, but your live-in fiancé expects you to do most of the housework, as his mom did. What do you do?
    (a) Male
    (b) Narcissistic
    (c) Female
    You don't need to fight or capitulate. You need only to gently say no to what does not feel good to you. Either he will negotiate or he won't, and if he won't, you can end the relationship.

12. Your boyfriend earns twice as much as you do but expects you to share 50-50 on dates. What do you do?
    (a) Male
    (b) Narcissistic
    (c) Female
    A tug of war over 50-50 is unromantic. Each of you deserves to date or be dated and have the tab paid by the initiator. Masculine men and women often initiate more dates than feminine men or women.

13. You have a boyfriend, and you travel a great deal for your work. What do you do?
    (a) Female
    (b) Male
    (c) Narcissistic
    Trustworthy socializing with the opposite sex is a sign of inner security on both sides. Sexualizing is forbidden but not socializing. Ex-lovers are dangerous as friends. Don't socialize with them.

14. Your boyfriend has been passed over for a promotion at his company. You have been invited to a company social event. What do you do?

(a) Male
(b) Narcissistic
(c) Female

Respecting your man's right to take care of himself is feminine. Taking care of him is masculine. Make sure he agrees first.

15. Both you and your boyfriend work long hours during the week and have little time for sex. What do you do?
    (a) Female
    (b) Narcissistic
    (c) Male

When you initiate sex verbally or physically, you run the risk of having sexual problems in performance. You can say no to what you don't want, but you'd better have an agreement from him first before you place him in the female receptive role.

If you have scored mostly MALE, decide if you really want to be the male. If you do, you must find a feminine man or woman. If not, you must *choose* to become more FEMALE.

If you have scored mostly FEMALE, you can mate with a masculine man or woman. Still, you should note where you have scored MALE and become more FEMALE in these areas, or risk conflict.

If you have scored mostly NARCISSISTIC, decide whether you wish to be MALE or FEMALE. If you don't *choose* to become either MALE or FEMALE, you will probably be unable to intimately mate.

MALENESS—Using logic primarily, and how you feel secondarily.

FEMALENESS—Using feelings primarily, and what you think secondarily.

NARCISSISTIC—Trying to use logic and feelings *equally*, which ultimately neutralizes both and ends intimacy through competitive conflict.

CHAPTER 6

What Masculine Men Want from Feminine Women

(*And What You Have to Understand About Masculine Men to Get What You Want*)

I f (based on my system), you choose to be the "feminine" energy in a relationship, it means that you will be looking for certain qualities from that "masculine" man who will best complement you, and he will be likewise expecting certain qualities from you. This chapter will distill his qualities and then guide you through your own corresponding role.

The "male" energy is the giving, initiating, leading, active partner, who elicits surrender, receptivity, and bonding from his partner. When the masculine energy gives, protects, and cherishes, he is penetrating the other's defenses to surrender to the pleasure of the relationship.

A masculine man is a natural developer of anything that he sees, and that includes a piece of land or a woman. With a woman, he thinks, *She is going to be so great if we just do this or that, and I'll show her how.*

Therefore, one of the most important qualities your masculine man will look for from you is joyous receptivity. By this I mean not only that he will expect you to receive gifts with joy, but also the things that don't feel too good, such as how-to-do-it messages. A man does not want to fight tooth and nail to get a thought into your thick skull. He wants you to be receptive to his opinions, suggestions, and plans.

Although you must respect your masculine man, you will not try to earn his respect. Instead, you will want him to cherish your feelings. Unfortunately, the more you intimidate a masculine man with your respectability, the less he will be able to see you as sexually desirable. Men with masculine-based energy systems tend to want to make love to women who want to be cherished, rather than women who want to be respected.

A second thing that a man wants from a woman is that she be available for him. That is why if you are a career woman instead of a woman with a career, your time will be limited, and you will not be compatible with a masculine man. A masculine man will want you to be available for him to play with and to have sex with, and he will want you to be responsive to his lovemaking, because he is not just a taker who is in it for his own pleasure. He wants to give you pleasure so that you will totally surrender to him. He will take particular joy in making you feel wonderful by bringing you to orgasm.

Feminine women surrender and bond to men through their bodies, through making love. When a woman gives her body to a man, there is a strong chance that she is going to become bonded to him—even after only one good sexual encounter. For this reason, it's easy to bond to the *wrong man*. A masculine man knows that if he gets into your knickers long enough and pleasures you, you're his. Before sex, he may have been a monster, but all of a sudden, after (good) sex, he gets better-looking and nicer. But what is really happening is that he is pleasing you, and you are rationalizing away his negative elements. Don't do it.

The basic qualities you will be looking for from your masculine man are that he be joyously generous, physically protective, and willing to cherish *your* painful feelings before his own.

Generosity is a very basic trait in a masculine man. If he has money to spend, he will do so joyously. He will not ask you to pay your way. If he invites you out for a date or for a trip, he will assume the responsibility for paying. Masculine men see their money as a way to have fun, not exert control. If they have it to spend, they do so with pleasure. Money is just the scorecard for the game; it is not the goal of a man's life.

A masculine man will want to provide money so that you will feel safe and secure, and so that you can enjoy life, especially after you marry. He will show his love by taking care of his money-making career. He knows that if he slacks off in the area of money-making, he risks the loss of respect for himself.

In contrast, as a feminine-energy woman, you will be more relationship-oriented. You will not have career and money as your first goals; therefore you will *need* a masculine man to give you status (marriage) and security. You will want him to pay the bills while you are having babies, while you are upgrading your career skills when the kids are little so that later you can return to your career. That way, between the two of you, work and relationships are balanced.

If, however, you make the mistake of allowing your man to view your career as "equal" to his, or even more important, you will rarely have the option of quitting for a baby or a cherished wish to follow your education.

A masculine man must be passionate about his work. It doesn't matter if he is a bank president or the janitor. A man with a boring job that does not excite his enthusiasm and creativity will not earn respect from you.

To maintain your respect, your masculine man will act in a disciplined manner, physically, mentally, and emotionally. If he binges on food, drink, drugs, or sex, or becomes a workaholic or emotionally binges on rages and violence, you will lose respect for him and inevitably be unable to be sexually responsive.

A man will maintain his woman's respect by making and keeping his commitments to the best of his ability. Any sloppiness with commitments will indicate that he doesn't cherish your feelings and wants his feelings cherished instead.

Narcissistic people always want to be respected *and* cherished, so if they fail to make or keep commitments, whether big or small, they want their behavior to be accepted and not confronted. But a woman with such a man will soon feel uncherished and quickly lose respect for him.

It is important that you do not rationalize away your feelings in favor of his. If he is the masculine energy and you are the feminine, it is his job to cherish *your* feelings ahead of his own. Unfortunately, a feminine woman who is sexually bonded to her man will often bend over backward to give him another chance, or make excuses for him, or delay confronting him when his priorities have slipped into selfishness. This is a big mistake. As soon as you perceive your man slipping, you must talk to him about your negative feelings, in order for the relationship to function smoothly.

Of course, at the same time you are watching to see how your masculine man is handling his priorities, he is watching to see how you are handling yours. Are you listening to his ideas? Are you fighting him for power and respect? Do you either break commitments or fail to make them? Do you fail to appreciate what he does to please you? Do you "give back" love, affection, time, and sensuous sexuality?

A masculine man must know what he thinks and wants. Knowing what he thinks and wants allows him to focus better, and a focused, thinking masculine man will act decisively, which will elicit respect from you, his feminine woman. He will say, "We're going to go there. We're going to do this. I'm going to get that job. I'm going to build this house. I'm going to provide for you. How do you feel about that?" And you will tell him how you feel, whether it be positive or negative. Of course, in order to get what you want, you must give your man what he wants, unless what he wants is immoral or unethical or causes you discomfort. You cannot use power plays, because in the long run, they don't work. The big error many feminine women make is to manipulate their men into giving back instead of waiting for their men to give first so they can give back.

Although you will want your masculine man to lead, you will not like being controlled, and sometimes it does feel like a man just wants to control you. If you find yourself in this situation, my suggestion is to say something like "I'm not comfortable doing this your way. Do you have another suggestion that might 'feel' better to me?"

If you speak to him this way, I can almost promise you that your masculine man will be happy to oblige, because it means that he is cherishing your negative feelings ahead of his own. By putting your feelings before his own, he is showing his commitment to you, and this will allow you to respect him and follow his lead.

Feminine women literally gush painful feelings verbally, and they need to know that all those painful feelings will be accepted, even if not approved of, by their men. Masculine-energy men like to nurture their loved ones. Their own internal feminine aspect wishes to empathize and share. They are not "macho men" out of touch with their feelings and unwilling to be open to another's pain. Instead, a masculine man is confident that he can cherish his woman until a solution can be found. He does not run away from her pain, nor does he expect her to handle it alone.

The problem is that sometimes your testosterone-based, level-headed masculine man will be annoyed with you at just the time you need his cherishing, because you are not as logical as he expects you to be. Often, the assumed-to-be "logical" words you are screaming at the top of your lungs are meaningless, and what you are really saying is "I'm scared. I feel jealous. I feel sad. I feel confused." This often results in conflict and argument, which can lead to the destruction of the relationship.

But what if your man doesn't even say a word at a time like that, but just hugs you, even though you are hostile. Then you and he can achieve communication. He has cherished your feelings, and you can relax and reconnect with your "smart" self and talk rationally. For a masculine man to say, "Honey, I hear your pain, but I haven't got a clear idea of what you're in pain about. Can you talk more about it?" is heaven on earth for a feminine woman.

Here is a pledge that I ask the masculine men at my seminars to take:

"I PROMISE TO CHERISH THE WOMEN, KIDS, AND ANIMALS IN MY LIFE, EVEN WHEN THEY ARE IRRATIONAL, IRRITATING, AND TOTALLY ILLOGICAL."

Here is one for the women:

"I PROMISE TO RESPECT MY CHOSEN MAN AND HIS THOUGHTS, SUGGESTIONS, IDEAS, AND PLANS, EVEN WHEN I KNOW I'M SMARTER AND CAN DO IT BETTER."

As a feminine woman, you will also want your masculine man to give you protection in the world. You will not want to have complete responsibility for your own welfare. You will not want to kick your own tires, change your own transmission oil, or check out strange sounds in the night. A masculine man will want to put his body between danger and his loved ones. He won't expect or assume that you can take care of yourself. Equality between the sexes in a love affair is not the masculine way.

A woman surrenders through her body, and a man surrenders when he makes a commitment. When he marries, he gives up irresponsibility and takes on the responsibility of his woman and everybody she loves, and she gives up her independence.

Does that mean that she gives up her sense of self, or that she doesn't have any rights? No. It just means she cannot remain physically, mentally, or emotionally independent. She can be what I call "undependent," which is dependent at home and independent at work.

The undependent feminine woman is dependent on a man in the categories where he has preference, usually in things that affect his role as financial provider, such as where they live and how they handle money, as well as love, affection, time, and sex.

An undependent woman does not need to codesign a budget. She trusts and respects her man and implements his design. If it doesn't work for her, she respectfully tells him how she feels, but she does not attempt to take over as if she could do it better. She defers to him for the "team's sake." A masculine man calls the plays, and she helps him implement them so that the "team" wins even if every player had to compromise some individual spontaneity and creativity along the way.

Likewise, the "undependent" man with a masculine-based energy system knows he has a right to his friends, his career, and hobbies and doesn't let a woman intimidate him out of them. An undependent, feminine woman has the same rights. Balancing and compromising are necessary to achieve these goals.

After they are married, he might stay home with the kids while she goes to a night class. Maybe she supports him playing golf on Sunday morning with the guys, while he works it into the budget that she can visit her family out of state. She understands that he needs to socialize with clients at times, and he understands that she might like to go out with the "girls."

Not every woman wants to do what is necessary to be the feminine energy. It can be difficult to defer and suppress a need to control and instead be patient and passive. But this is what it takes to be with a masculine man. If you don't want to curtail your male energy, there are feminine men who will follow your lead. Choose your style!

After they had been together for a few months, Althea was sure that Joseph loved her. He tried to please her in small and large ways. She had never experienced such tender love so freely given, and soon she became accustomed to it. Everything was perfect, except the problem she had with his career.

Joseph was a cameraman for a major studio in L.A., and his hours were difficult. When he was shooting a picture, he might be on the set until 2:00 A.M. Going on location took him away for weeks at a time.

At first Althea did not complain about his hours, because she was afraid to turn him off by driving him away, but after nine months she felt confident about his commitment and began giving him a hard time, knowing full well that Joseph could do little about his hours, and that his work was very important to him.

At first he listened and comforted her by reminding her he was saving money for her engagement ring, but as time passed,

Joseph saw that cherishing Althea did little good. She wanted to control his career, and he would not have it. He warned her that he was running out of patience, and when she continued to complain, he left.

Althea was devastated. She thought he had needed her more than anything and could not leave. *Wrong!* Joseph was willing to share himself and his life but was not willing to be controlled. Althea needed to learn how to respect a man.

The sad thing is, once they leave, masculine men tend to slam the door on intimacy with the woman they just left. They can be friends but rarely lovers again. As one man told me, "Once a deal falls out of escrow, I leave it and go on. The connection is broken."

CHAPTER 7

What Masculine-Energy Women Want from Feminine-Energy Men

(And What You Have to Give Them to Get What You Want)

S o you like your career, money, power, and prestige, and you also want a man. How do you live a balanced life? This chapter is for you. You are not a "freak," and your alternative style *will* work for you, as long as you decide to be the dynamic, masculine, giving energy in a relationship and choose a receptive, feminine-energy man who is willing to bring you his loving and sensual skills to make life fun for you both.

Masculine energy likes to make money and wield power and prestige. Feminine energy likes to make love, build families, and play.

A healthy, sensitive masculine-energy woman is generous, and will make certain, to the best of her ability, that her man is always comfortable and not humiliated over the issue of money. If you control the money, your sensitive, feminine-energy man may feel uncomfortable with you paying the bill at a restaurant. He may ask that you support his manhood by allowing him his discretionary funds for entertainment and gifts. That is as it should be. Each person in a relationship needs to be able to function financially independently of the other in order to be an adult. Whenever one person must ask the other for money, problems arise, producing resentments that corrode the relationship.

Making money and controlling money are two different issues. Although you as a masculine-energy woman may be the prime source of financial security and status within the relationship, and he the secondary source, he still may be the better comptroller. This depends on the natural or educated skills of the individuals. If you are the money-maker, it is your right to decide who controls the gross earnings, investments, and retirement plans, whether it be you, your husband, or a professional money manager, because you have worked hard to earn it. Also, within the marriage, a certain amount of money must be allocated from the gross earned to the family, and someone also must see to it that this is done efficiently, effectively, and economically. That is also something to be decided between both of you, based on each of your aptitudes and desires. Too many women in the glow of early love abdicate their responsibility for the money they earn to their man in a false and destructive attempt at being a feminine woman. Don't you do it. I have observed that an unhealthy masculine-energy-based woman who holds the purse strings will often try to humiliate her man by flaunting her "power and control."

As a masculine-energy-based woman, you must be generous with your time, sex, affection, and love, as well as your money. If you have a choice between work and play, choose to play with your man rather than work at the office. Schedule your work with an eye toward balancing work and play and, if possible, avoid taking work home. What cannot be done at the office probably is a sign of inefficient time management. Workaholism is the potential killer of the relationship between a masculine woman and her feminine man.

As the "masculine" energy, you must appreciate and cherish your man's gentle, sensual qualities, without bearing him resentment or losing respect for him. As I said earlier, choosing to be feminine does not mean being weak. On the contrary, a feminine-energy man must be secure enough in himself that he respects your leadership and does not resent you for it or try to undermine you competitively, as a masculine man might. He enjoys the excitement of your dynamic self and does not feel threatened by your brightness and successes in the world. He will be turned on by your power and your achievements outside the home, just as a masculine man is excited by a feminine woman's achievements inside the home. He pays his way by making life fun for you after a hard day's work and likes your bringing home the money, power, and prestige to him, for his pleasure.

Of course, if you are the major breadwinner, you will expect him to make your life more fun and easier for you after work. He might well see to it that your home looks good and runs well, and he will often make the social decisions and reservations that will create fun for you after work.

One sign of a secure feminine-energy man is that he will respect your decisions about your money and career, accept your directions, and, to the best of his abilities, assist you in staying healthy, having fun, and making the most of your wonderful talents and skills. He will intuitively feel your sensitive "little girl" side and cherish it. He will have integrated his "feminine" into his masculine personality and will be able to exhibit sensitivity and yield to your needs without resenting it. He will be secure in his relationship with you. He is your support system and loves you the way you are and the way the relationship balances.

He can accept your going out of town on business. Remember, even if he has his own job or career, he supports yours as the main one. If you need to move, he goes happily and not competitively, and he laughs off the ridicule that macho types throw at him.

If you are the masculine energy, he must be receptive to your ideas and be available to you physically, mentally, and emotionally. On your side, you must seek out and listen to what he needs to feel cherished. If you are using a feminine man only as a sex machine or as a baby-sitter who keeps house, you are misusing your masculine energy, which is supposed to give, protect, and cherish.

A man in this situation must not rationalize away being abused and used. He must leave his woman if necessary, if only to "get her attention." Too often gentle men are seen as weak. Leaving will cure that. A masculine woman must feel the loneliness of her man being gone, because I promise you, no matter what sex you are, making money is not as much fun as making love. If you think making money is more fun, *don't marry*.

As in all relationships that are chemically erotic, complements attract. As a masculine woman, you will complement a feminine man, and be chemically attracted to him, just as he is to you. You like his sensitive, sensuous, sexual side, and he likes your dynamic, sensuous, sexual side.

Often you will actively seek him out by *talking first to him*. You will not wait passively for him to speak. His sensitivity may mean he will not want to risk rejection from such a seemingly "powerful" woman. Someone has got to be the "left-lobed" talker, and if you want to be the masculine energy, it might as well be you.

Masculine women have a lot of sexual energy, and feminine men enjoy assertive sexual women, unlike masculine men who see this as a performance demand. Feminine men turn on to power in a woman.

But sex may be a problem for some masculine women. Often a masculine woman has difficulty ceasing to be primarily "rational" and loosening up. Having a loving, sexy encounter with a feminine man will do this immediately. In fact, for some masculine women, sex is their only pleasurable outlet for pent-up physical needs. Such women like polygamous, uncommitted sex with unavailable men. It is safer and keeps them independent.

These women can find men who will be partners for them because they are "low-maintenance" females, but, of course, they may attract men who feed off them. One of the ways to avoid such men is to avoid casual sex.

Just because you are a masculine woman and feel "in control" of the relationship does not mean that you can have casual sex like a masculine man. Unless you are totally "in your head" and out of your body, you will be affected by the hormone oxytocin.

As I said earlier, casual, noncontracted sex in a normal woman triggers a bonding that can verge on physical addiction. This is due to a sexually stimulated hormone called oxytocin, which is predominant in females and which triggers orgasm. Over a period of time, you, too, can "bond" physically to the man you're having sex with. It may take you longer than a feminine-energy woman, but when you do bond, it could become an addiction and cause illness and loss of your ability to work.

So, just like a more feminine woman, you must check out your man before making love to him. Take time to find the right man so that you can have both a career and a loving partner.

Make certain he agrees to your long-term goals, and don't have sex until you know the commitment boundaries and feel good about them. Make sure he is not a bingeing sex addict, gratifying his feminine need to feel good at any cost, even if the cost to both of you is AIDS.

After chemical attraction, negotiation is the prime ingredient in a successful relationship between a masculine woman and a feminine man, because most likely both of you will have careers you must attend to successfully, *and* you both have the need to be intimate after work. Therefore, you must negotiate how you spend your time, where you live, how you share home and family responsibilities, who, and in what way, will handle the money, investments, bill-paying, and especially how you will play together.

As a masculine woman, you must say what you think and want and ask your man how he feels about what is going on in your dual careers, shared child care, and family life. If he withholds telling you how he feels and does not say no to what he does not want, he is weak. But feminine men need not be weak. They need only feel good about being sensitive, and they are able to tell you how they feel in a forthright manner.

If your man doesn't like something that is going on and tells you so, you must listen and be willing to negotiate. You must not intimidate him with logical arguments, taking advantage of his willingness to compromise by saying, "If you respected me, you would agree to what I want."

At the same time, a feminine man will ask you about your wants and show his feelings about them, so that you can be a "we" and negotiate for mutual benefit. He will avoid seducing you away from your career goals by putting his feelings negatively against them: "If you really loved me, you wouldn't go," etc.

As a masculine woman, you are still an estrogen-based, feeling person who just happens to be a career woman rather than a woman with a career. This means you will still feel hurt if your man shows you that he cannot be a committed adult. When you ask him to do something with you, or for you, he has to keep his word and not go passive-aggressive with resentment, as "little boy" men do. And you must keep your commitments to him.

If what I have said here fits you, then go for it. Never mind what your mother, sister, and friends say about getting a powerful man to marry you. You have probably tried "powerful" men, single and married, and they don't work for you. You bump into them, or need to shut down who you really are, and you don't feel good about it.

The most prevalent problem that masculine women have is embarrassment over their role of leader in the relationship. Having an alternative lifestyle and being in the minority can push a masculine woman into confusion and anger.

One way she acts this out is that after being in a long-term or marital relationship with a feminine man, she may arbitrarily decide that it is time for him to become the money-making head of the household and that she will stay home.

If she chooses to do this based on negative feelings, it *never* works. She will quickly resent quitting her good job and her loss of status, money, and control. However, her feminine man may be thrown into the masculine world where he may find he likes it, now that he has a wife and kids and a little stability in his life. Feminine men bloom wonderfully around a strong woman and often become very masculine as time goes by. The problem then is that now both want to be the masculine energy, and conflict results. If, on the other hand, the feminine man does not like the "masculine" role he has been thrown into, he well might fail or leave her to find another woman.

I have seen masculine women and feminine men switch roles as they get older, just as the masculine man retires and his wife goes back to school or work. As long as they complement each other, it can work.

There is a gentle, sensitive, often shy man out there who is waiting for you to find him. Open your eyes and look for him. He is often overlooked by women as not a "real man." But he is, in his own fun way. Remember that to have a loving, sexual, committed relationship, all you need is one respectful, caring person and one cherished, fun person, and it doesn't matter which is which.

I ask the women at my seminars who have chosen to be the "masculine" energy to take this pledge:

"I PROMISE TO GIVE, PROTECT, AND CHERISH THE FEELINGS OF MY FEMININE MAN, EVEN WHEN HE IS IRRATIONAL, ILLOGICAL, AND IRRITATING, AS LONG AS HE GIVES BACK TO ME, SENSUALLY AND SEXUALLY."

HARRIET

Harriet, an attractive brunette novelist and magazine writer, grew up in a family of strong women—her grandmothers on both sides were writers, her aunt was a lawyer, and her mother an actress who performed and taught drama and public speaking. But her father had a traditional male role as the "breadwinner," and his word was law. He was stern and distant, and never, as her friends' fathers did, encouraged her femininity or treated her differently from her brother.

She had only one serious relationship with a man who was pursuing a successful corporate career. The argument that ended the relationship was over a trivial matter, but the underlying issue was that Harriet didn't feel the man was taking her opinion seriously enough. After that, she dated the men who were *really* attractive to her: T-shirt and jeans types, usually handsome, often involved in the arts, nontraditional in their thinking and style, invariably not concerned about "getting ahead," and always respectful of her intelligence. She was usually more successful than they, earning enough money to get the kind of apartment she wanted, taking herself on trips, buying the clothes she desired.

On their first date, Eric, a journalist and the man she eventually married, told her that he didn't make much money. Although Harriet appreciated him mentioning it, she didn't much care.

On the second date, they went to dinner at a friend's house: She arrived first and noticed when he came to the door that he had brought wine. He talked easily with the host before coming over to her; then he sat down next to her, patted her knee, and gave her a wink. He was flirtatious, sociable, and a bit of a dilettante, and, to her amazement, he found the fact that she had been an honor student and a Goody Two-shoes not only interesting but something to boast to other people about.

When they dated, she usually paid, or they split the check. When they moved in together, they used her credit references to secure the lease, and she paid for the move.

They have been married for twelve years, and in that time Harriet, who started out earning slightly more than Eric, has become the complete breadwinner now that Eric stays at home with their eight-year-old son and works on his novel. Since Harriet realizes that she would have to pay the basic costs of living if she lived alone, she willingly covers these costs. Her only request is that Eric earn enough to give him walking-around money, which he does, and which helps his self-respect.

Eric brings spontaneity, enthusiasm, and unpredictability to their relationship, as well as sensuality and sexuality. She finds him attractive and vital. He is a loving father to their child. Obviously, he enjoys the comfort and security that she provides, and when he talks about her, it is with respect and pride.

If they need something for the apartment, if she or he or their son needs clothes, she buys them and doesn't care about getting things in return, yet she treasures the sentimental notes and cards Eric sends her on her birthday, Valentine's Day, and at Christmas.

When they go to some parties, Harriet says she feels as if she should be hanging out with the men, because she doesn't feel like "one of the girls"—except in Eric's presence. Although he is proud of her for her competence, he is still flirtatious with her, a quality she never got from her father and rarely inspired in anyone else. Harriet thinks she has got a pretty good deal, and Eric thinks that he has, too.

PART TWO

HOW TO ATTRACT A MAN

CHAPTER 8

Flirt to Attract

If you want to "attract" a masculine-energy male, you must be "seen" as a sex object. You take care of your body, dress sensuously, fix your hair and makeup, go where men are, catch "his" eye, and signal your interest and availability (the Five-Second Flirt Technique) so he won't be afraid to approach you. Smile, don't talk. If you speak first, you're the better man.

What a man and a woman communicate during their initial contact is so crucial that it will determine whether they will remain strangers or become lifetime mates. Males and females flirt in different ways, so before you go out there to attract a mate, decide whether you are the male or the female energy.

PACKAGING YOUR FEMININITY

Barbara, an attractive and confident-looking travel industry executive, came onstage at one of my seminars, admitting that men rarely asked her out. She was charming, clever, and interesting, but although she met lots of men through her work, she almost never dated, and she was completely mystified as to why.

But the moment I saw her, I realized that as a seductive female, Barbara was a visual washout. Although pretty, she was dressed that evening in a trendy but shapeless pantsuit, and she wore little makeup. I knew that Barbara badly needed to be validated as a woman.

I asked whether she wanted to be the male or the female energy. "The female," she said quickly. "In that case," I replied, "I suggest you wear this outfit only when you want comfort above everything—even getting a man. Otherwise, I suggest you change your fashion look in order to present yourself as a sensuous-looking woman *all the time*."

"But I don't want to be seen as a sex object," she said adamantly. "I've worked hard to get where I am. I want to be respected as a person."

Barbara went on to tell me that she didn't want a man who was interested in the way a woman looked. She wanted one who could see inside, right through to her soul. I told Barbara that masculine men aren't sexually attracted to a woman's soul, but to a woman's physical magnetism. When a man approaches a woman, he first of all wants to see if he can have a good time with her, and that includes physical gratification. A woman may not want to be seen as a sex object, but the truth is, she has to be if she wants to attract a man.

By the end of the seminar, Barbara had agreed to change her visual presentation. At home later that night, she went through her closet, picking out her outfit for the next day, one that seemed both appropriate for the office and feminine, and she discarded the clothes that seemed to deliberately deny her femaleness.

By the time she left for work the next morning, she had totally changed her look. Her hair was loose, her makeup was artfully applied, and instead of a baggy slacks suit, she wore a black silk blouse, short black skirt, black stockings, and pumps, topped off by a pink formfitting jacket she hadn't worn in years. She looked both well-dressed and sensually appealing. And although she felt vulnerable, she was able to smile in the elevator at her neighbor, an attractive bachelor. He asked her out to dinner before their elevator reached the lobby.

That day turned out to be one of the most important of Barbara's life. The response to the way she now looked, including compliments from her co-workers, kicked off a new understanding of how much she had been inappropriately dressed for man-hunting. "Trendy" and "chic" can be statements of wealth and can appeal to other females, but often they are not sexually attractive to men. Barbara had been hiding behind her masculine clothes and had never really understood what she was doing.

This change in body-language communication through clothes was a new beginning for Barbara, the start of actualizing her dreams. Now she was dressing to attract a man and to find love.

YOU DON'T HAVE TO BE PERFECT

I know that you want to be loved for yourself, and maybe, someday, your man will love you this way, shortcomings and all. But right now, your best chance of getting him in the first place is by looking the very best you can, and transforming yourself into the most attractive-looking, lovable, and sensuous woman you can be.

You must pay attention to your body. Try to eat well and work out as much as you can, no matter what age you are. Your body is a reflection of your soul and your sanity. It's a statement of how much in control of yourself you are. If a woman doesn't take care of her body, if she can live in a messy environment, she is not in touch with her feelings as a woman.

You must pay attention to your grooming. Like it or not, you *are* judged by the way you look. If you have a heart of gold but look like a slob, you are putting yourself at a distinct disadvantage, so you must think about why you are trying to sabotage your chances at romance.

First impressions cannot be made a second time. Seduce his eyes; don't sabotage. Try to see this from *his* point of view. Would you be attracted to a man who looked sloppy and unkempt?

But don't be too hard on yourself. Remember that we are all human, and imperfect, so even if you are ten pounds overweight or you hate your nose, or your hair is too straight or too curly, take heart. Your being beautiful is not really a requirement for a man to commit to a long-term relationship with you. Men know that if a woman's body is well-kept and healthy, the rest is a gift from the gods. When they're playing for keeps, men are much more attracted to a loving personality than to perfection. A beautiful woman without an amiable personality will usually drive her man away quickly. In the long run, a man wants a woman who is lovable.

Take time to create your most attractive hairdo, your prettiest makeup, get into your sexiest dress, and put on an inviting smile. You want to overwhelm a man's senses by looking good, tasting good, smelling good, feeling good, and sounding good—but, primarily, looking good. Leave those baggy, masculine, or conservative clothes at home, because they signal a lack of sexuality, and you want to signal him that you *are* desirable. You may choose to turn him down when he makes his move, but you do want him to make the move, don't you?

The bottom line is: Go with what you've got, and go for the best you can get. Remember, even though your image of him is one of perfection, let's face it, he's not going to be perfect, and neither are you.

MARKETING YOUR FEMININITY

Now that you look great, where do you find "him"? It's simple. Start by going where the men are.

I can't tell you how many women I meet who will stop at nothing to further their careers, but though they complain about being alone, think that going out and looking for a man is degrading. They think it makes them look desperate. *They are wrong*. These days you must go out and hunt for romance with the same skill and determination you would muster to look for a job or an apartment.

If you don't like being alone, do something about it. Don't stay home and expect a man to come down your chimney like Santa Claus. It's footwork that counts . . . being out there, among the people—at parties, supermarkets, theater lines, parks, beaches, restaurants, adult education classes, and ball games—ready, willing, and *able* to flirt.

If you choose to be the feminine-energy woman, dress sensuously, but of course take into account the style that suits you best—cute, sleek, feminine. Sex appeal doesn't mean frilly, girly, or happy homemaker. It is an individual decision. Package yourself to bring out *your* sensual attributes in a tasteful but alluring manner. There are professional image makers out there who can help you if you have the money, but they aren't needed if you don't. As long as there are magazines, you can cut out pictures of styles you think would enhance your sexual look. Wear clothes that reveal your curves and are sensuous to touch. Make sure your hair is well-cut as well as silky to the touch. The colors you choose should suit your skin tone and personality. Possibly you could ask a friend to come with you to a fabric store and drape cloth over a white blouse or T-shirt near your face. Your friend can tell you what enhances and what doesn't. Color attracts a man's gaze and will bring him toward you.

Most department stores have face-makeup sessions to sell their products. If you don't have money, get a free one, and write down what the saleswoman says about your face. Don't forget about secondhand consignment shops, especially in rich areas where wealthy women discard last year's wardrobes. Most assistance leagues have thrift stores with *great* buys in clothes, purses, shoes, and accessories. With or without money, you can enhance your sensual look. Make the effort—it is worth it!

Go out to at least one social event each week, and when there, flirt just for fun. In the beginning, you will be nervous and clumsy. I suggest you practice some "throwaway" experiences such as flirting in an elevator when you go to see your doctor or dentist. Flirt in the checkout line of a big grocery store where you don't keep seeing the same people every day. Think of these as loosening-up or stretching experiences for the "big run," i.e., the office party, the wedding reception, the class reunion—places where you will be known and where first impressions will count.

I always recommend airports for beginners, because they are

a place where people are generally stranded without their loved ones, and they want some kind of human interaction of a non-dangerous type. Take a briefcase so you look like you're going somewhere, and don't worry whether the man you choose is married, because you are only practicing flirting. No phone number exchanges, no dinner dates made, nothing except pulling him toward you to say some innocuous things for a moment. See how many men you can magnetize in an hour. Maybe you and a friend can compete in this game.

If possible, date several (at least three) different men, in order not to focus obsessively on one, and remember not to call or in any way pursue a man, because that is male behavior, and you have chosen to be the female. You want to draw a man toward you. If you change systems in midstream, you are signaling that you want to be a narcissistic single woman who doesn't care if she confuses men and drives them away from a long-term stable commitment.

When you are ready to do some serious flirting, think about the qualities you want in a man. If it's important for him to share your love of classical music, by all means order Philharmonic tickets right now, but this time, instead of going just for Mozart, go to flirt as well. If you feel it's important for him to be athletic, flirt at your gym or tennis court or golf course or jogging track, or while biking, walking, or doing whatever sport you do. If his religion or political party is important, then flirt at church or a political meeting. Go where you go naturally, but try to view it as a pool of potential mates.

Now, you might say you have been going to the Philharmonic for years—maybe alone, probably with a friend—hoping that a charming, attractive, successful single man of the right age and religious persuasion will see you, approach you, and ask you out, without your having to do a thing.

Instead, what usually happens is that you go to the lobby during intermission and stand around like everybody else. Occasionally, a man you think is adorable looks your way and seems as though he wants to come over and talk to you. You whisper—or maybe pray—to yourself, "Please cross the room," but he hesitates. You want to let him know you're interested, but you feel paralyzed by the attraction and by your strong emotions. So instead of looking at him, you engage in an animated conversation with your friend.

If he does look your way, you're probably so nervous from your fear of rejection that you turn away. That's it. The bell rings, and you go back to your seat. Another missed opportunity.

Don't think you are the only person in the world who does this. I've seen women who are fearless powerhouses in the business world become petrified when they are faced with a strange man to whom they are sexually attracted.

For months, Mary, a hairdresser, had been badgered by her friend Lorraine to go out in the evening with her to see if they could meet some attractive men. Mary wanted to meet someone with whom she could make a commitment, so she agreed to meet Lorraine for a drink at a small neighborhood café that featured a jazz group she especially liked.

By the time they arrived, the room was already crowded, and Mary and Lorraine were lucky to find a small table against the wall near the stage. As soon as they sat down, Mary noticed an attractive man intently listening and moving to the music, and then, between sets, talking enthusiastically to his friends. She liked his looks and his passion for jazz. But he seemed not to know she was there.

David was a telephone repairman, with a penchant for jazz and backpacking and a love of American history, who wanted most in life to marry and settle down. He had many good friends, but although he was warm and easygoing, when it came to women, David would usually freeze up, held back by his own shyness.

That's what was happening now. David in fact had been aware of Mary from the moment she had come into the room, but he just couldn't look directly at her. David's friend Ted told him that Mary kept glancing his way. David was pleased. Do I go over, or not? he wondered, wanting to but, as usual, doing nothing.

Finally, before the last set began, he managed to turn to Mary, and for a moment, their eyes met. Mary felt a surge of heat go through her, but she was so embarrassed by her own vulnerability and desire that she became nervous and quickly looked away from David, who in turn felt rejected.

"Why doesn't he come over?" Mary whispered to Lorraine in frustration.

"You go over and say hello to him," was her friend's advice, but Mary didn't move. She felt she simply could not go over to a strange man.

Then David's friend Ted glanced toward Mary, and she managed to give him a faint smile. This only worsened matters because David saw Mary smiling at Ted and felt hurt.

"Just go over and talk to her," Ted advised David, when he saw the look on his face. "What have you got to lose?"

"She doesn't like me," replied David, "she likes you."

"Me? She's been looking at you all night."

"Maybe," replied David, "but she looked away from me—and she smiled at you."

Both David and Mary went home alone that night, each feeling rejected and each thinking about the other. Had she only followed my Five-Second Flirt Technique, she would have magnetized David to her and perhaps begun the relationship each of them wanted.

MY FIVE-SECOND FLIRT TECHNIQUE

My technique is easy. It's the way you invite him by your own body language to come across the room and ask you out. You don't do anything more than smile, but if you do this properly, I promise you will have results.

The first thing you want to do is to get into his line of sight. When you catch his eye, you must give him the most inviting and receptive look you can manage, for three seconds. Count them. Eye contact, eye contact, eye contact. No quick counts, no matter how nervous you get.

However, catching a man's eye for two or three seconds is

quite normal. It's when you continue to look at him for the fourth and fifth second that you indicate you're interested.

A second way you attract a man is with your mouth, but not to talk with it. You smile! Now you're being flirtatious. Now he knows that you're looking at, and are interested in, *him.*

By now, because you are flirting with a person you don't want to be rejected by, you are probably in a panic. Your mouth may be dry. This results in three potentially disastrous experiences: Your top lip starts curling (which I call "hung lip"), and your bottom lip starts quivering, and, even worse, perspiration drips down your blouse. For this reason, you should never flirt in silk, and try not to wear pastels. The rule is, never show sweat. It gives away everything.

But here's the good part. Even though you're certain that he is observing your meltdown, he isn't, because he is too busy with his own anxiety and fear of rejection. At that moment, his worst nightmare is that he will come over to you and say something stupid, and you will turn away.

So, if you live through this Five-Second Flirt Technique and you've managed to keep your mouth shut, more likely than not this man will walk over to you and start talking. He may say something bright or stupid, suave or naïve, but in effect he'll open the channel of conversation, and now you can begin to respond.

CHEMICAL ATTRACTION: IS IT FOR REAL?

Naturally, unless you are just flirting for practice, you flirt with the man who triggers a chemical reaction in you. Chemistry is not negotiable, but whom you flirt with is.

The initial attraction between two people is chemical. He turns you on. You turn him on. It doesn't matter if he is a truck driver or the president of General Motors, much older than you are or much younger. Chemistry is a body-to-body response. You can either act on it or forget it. But if you want to act on it, you have only two choices. You can take either the "male" role and chase men, *or* choose to be female and wait to be chased.

If you choose to be female, the way to get a man you are attracted to is by flirting. You choose him, then attract him to you.

SHE WHO FLIRTS FIRST IS FEMALE

Statistical research as well as anthropological studies show that even though a man might be attracted to a woman, before he can approach her, the sensitive part of him needs a signal from her that she is approachable and available and isn't going to reject him. Flirting is that signal.

The more passive a woman is, the more potent she is, because she attracts a man toward her. A woman is most erotic when she is magnetic. You pull a man close to you through your lovable exterior, your loving eyes and smile. You want him to be able to look into your eyes in order to see your gentleness and come after you. Women's eyes show kindness or cruelty. Flirting is a way to connect inside to outside. You want to smile at him so he can "see" your approachability. Remember, a man is a sensitive, loving human being who is probably scared to death of crossing over that magic circle to you, only to be made to feel like a fool. But cross it he must, if he is to take the masculine role.

FLIRTING WITH MR. WRONG

Often, even when we do flirt, we women are so afraid to expose ourselves to the man we're interested in that we flirt with the one next to him—whom we don't want—hoping that somehow the right one will notice how wonderful we are. The problem is that, like David (and most men), he has this weird idea that if you are flirting with the guy next to him, then *he's* the one you want. He doesn't realize that you're afraid of rejection. The worst part is that we usually attract that other guy, and then it takes us months to get free of him.

Do not avoid the man you are attracted to by rationalizing

that he is married or won't want you. During my weekly group seminars, I like to ask women to make this pledge:

"I PROMISE, ON MY HONOR, TO FLIRT WITH THE PERSON I TRULY WANT, NOT THE EASY ONE, FOR IT IS DIFFICULT TO GET RID OF THE EASY ONES."

This is not rocket science but simple chemistry. The man you are most terrified to flirt with is almost always the one who is most sexually attractive to you. Anxiety and tension are an integral part of the chemistry that causes the original attraction. True, it's no fun to flirt. We are doing it strictly to get results.

FOR FEMALES WHO CHOOSE THE MALE ROLE

If you have decided to be the male energy in the relationship, you, too, will need to package yourself properly. Get a car, heel your shoes, dress well, and look as though you are a responsible and financially solvent person.

For you, flirting is fairly straightforward. When you see a man you're interested in, you simply (I know it sounds simpler than it is!) walk over and begin talking to him, and, hopefully, your charm and personality will win him over. It doesn't matter what you say (within reason). You must walk over to him and begin to talk. Then, if he still interests you, you may ask for his telephone number or say you'd like to make a date. Then you can call him or send a note, send flowers, whatever—you do the pursuing.

Once you're on the date, don't forget that as with the feminine woman, the major sexual responder in a feminine man is his ears, which means that he wants to hear that you know how to pick a restaurant, order the wine, and pay the bill.

HE (OR SHE) WHO SPEAKS FIRST IS MALE

As I have said, it is in the very first moment of contact between two people that the male and the female roles are established. Since male energy is assertive and female energy passive, he who speaks first is male.

If you speak first, even accidentally, it sets a precedent that will continue for the rest of the relationship. So, you might as well sort this out in the beginning. Otherwise, it could take months before you figure out you've made the wrong choice.

You must remember this rule, especially if you are following the "feminine" role, because even a masculine man may hesitate in walking over to you, and that's when you have to endure the frustration of suppressing that voice crying within you, "Just go up to him and say, 'Hi, how are you?' " Instead, just look and smile and wait for him to say, "Hi," or something that indicates that he wants to go on with you.

Some men may wait for you to approach them, but unless you're willing to be the masculine energy in the relationship, don't do it. Don't make it easy for him. Being spoken to first is distracting to a man who is used to "seeing" whom he wants sexually and then going after her before he "hears" her invitation to connect sexually. Having "chasing space" is a turn-on for a masculine man. It is then that he begins to fall in love.

INVESTIGATING YOUR COMPATIBILITY (OR LEARNING HOW TO LISTEN)

Now that you've gotten him to walk over to you, you have two goals. First, you'll want to begin to see if he is as good as he seems, and second, you don't want to drive him away before you decide whether or not you want to keep him.

When Patty, a literary agent, saw Jerry, a psychoanalyst, waiting outside an evening computer class they had both signed up for, she was immediately attracted to him, and he to her. They began to talk, and soon they were in a lively discussion about the merits of different laser printers. After a few minutes, the conversation turned on a slight disagreement, which then escalated into a heated debate.

Patty won the argument but lost the guy. Without even thinking about it, Jerry had turned off to her by the time their class began. Patty didn't mean to turn him off. She didn't even know she *had* turned him off. She was just being herself, after a hard day of trying to sell her clients' books and making deals.

But Jerry had come from a hard day of work, too. All day he had listened to people's problems, and he was tired and maybe a little irritable, that is, until he saw Patty, who was so appealing—right up until the moment she opened up her mouth and started correcting him.

A man needs to feel respected by the woman he is sexually attracted to, but all too often we manage to screw the whole thing up by criticizing his opinions, arguing about his philosophies, and generally making ourselves obnoxious. The end result is that he never asks us out, and we think he's a jerk.

Being a sensual female means biting your lip now and then. Instead of competing intellectually with your man, try to keep quiet and let him do most of the talking. Find out if he's dull, married, weird, or terrific. Try to learn whether he's the head of a million-dollar corporation or an out-of-work bartender.

When you listen to him, you want to hear about his business, what his creative mode is, where he is putting his enthusiasm. You want to know: Does he change jobs every two weeks, does he gamble, is he misusing his resources? In order to respect a man, which is a turn-on for most women, you need to learn that he can provide you with a good time, a lifestyle that's comfortable, and if you want children, that he can provide a home for you and your children.

So instead of advice, try offering a man affection and respect. Be positive and supportive and encouraging about his ideas, his plans, his opinions. Have I gotten my point across?

If he asks you a question, you can answer anything that your intuition tells you to as long as you're responding to his lead and as long as you're talking about him and his goals and needs, not yours, unless asked.

If you ask a question, it can't be, "When can I see you again?" or "Can I have your number?" This signals that you want to pursue him.

All right, I know you may be cringing. But I never said finding the right mate was going to be easy. I just said it would be worth the effort.

Patty, the literary agent, has now changed her ways. She has learned that all people are "male" at work, but women who want to go female after work must leave their male side at the office, so that they can relate to a man in the sensitive, sensuous, and seductive ways that will bring them what they want.

If you want to be a "feminine" woman, you'll take at least an hour before or after work every day to do some activity that feels good and is fun for you, such as dancing, listening to music, communicating with nature, taking a bubble bath, eating a wonderful meal, having a massage—anything that allows you to practice the feminine principle of relatedness. If you go to the gym to work out and be healthy, you're not going there to be female. If you go to the gym to dance to music, to swim, or to lie around and talk to the girls, you are "going feminine."

The following is a pledge I ask "feminine-energy" women who come to my seminars to take:

"I PROMISE TO WASTE AT LEAST ONE HOUR EACH DAY OF MY LIFE, TASTING, TOUCHING, SEEING, SMELLING, AND HEARING, WITH NO PERFORMANCE IN MIND, AND I PROMISE TO SHARE THAT PROCESS ONCE A WEEK WITH ANOTHER HUMAN BEING, IN ORDER TO PRESERVE MY FEMININE ABILITY TO BE FEELING-CENTERED AND RELATIONSHIP-ORIENTED, SO HELP ME GOD!"

Patty learned how to do it. She used my "declawing" exercises, tried to keep her mouth relatively closed, and found herself an adorable attorney whom she is contemplating marrying.

If it can happen to Patty, it can happen to you.

Now I'm not saying you have to go against anything you strongly believe in, I'm just saying that you should look for areas of compromise. Accept that he may have a point of view worth hearing, then hear it and go with it, unless it is unethical or immoral, or it doesn't feel good to your body. Later, when you reach the negotiation stage of your relationship, you can suggest alternatives to anything that really bothers you.

Remember, if he isn't a man you can respect, he isn't the man for you.

EXIT MOVES
(OR, WHAT TO DO IF HE GIVES YOU HIS PHONE NUMBER)

Debbie, a pretty, dark-haired photographer, met Max, a political writer, at an environmental fund-raiser.

As they stood together waiting for the next speaker, Max told Debbie about a newspaper series he was writing, and she was moved by his values and idealism. Not only was he extremely attractive, with a thick head of curly hair and a full beard, but he seemed kind and sensitive and unattached.

Debbie was almost afraid to hope that Max would ask for her telephone number, but then, happily, he did suggest that they see each other again, only to reach into his jacket pocket and hand her his business card, suggesting that she give him a call.

You know what happened next. When Debbie finally got up the nerve to call Max, he said he was on the other line and that he would call back. When he didn't, she figured he had lost her number, so she called him again. But then he wasn't in, and she left a message on his answering machine. After that, she called a few more times, but never, it seemed, at the right time for Max, who kept asking that she call back—except for the one time when he did call back, dropped by her apartment, had sex with her, and never bothered to call again.

It took Debbie a long time to recover from that one, but she learned her lesson and the truth about men who give women their phone numbers.

When a man gives you his card, he is telling you that he wants you to pursue him. Some women believe that they are surrendering to a man's maleness by succumbing to his wish that they call him. But what they're surrendering to is his female side. And when you do call, what does he say? "I don't know about getting together, I'm kind of busy." Usually, he's just collecting scalps on his "little boy" totem pole.

So if he gives you his card, don't take it. Tell him you're not comfortable calling men, and give him yours. Then, wait for him to call you. Let him chase you, pursue you, woo you, and wow you—because that's his role, not yours. When a man requires a woman to give, he then becomes the female.

By the way, there is a time limit on how long you have to stand around talking to a man you've flirted with, waiting for him to ask for your number. I hesitate to give an exact time, in case five more minutes would have gotten him off the dime, but on the average if he hasn't made his move in roughly fifteen minutes and the energy has about gone out of the conversation, get ready to move on. You don't have to do a thing but look good, smell good, and sound good. The rest is up to him.

If he doesn't ask for your number, forget it. Don't take it personally. Don't fall into a black hole of despair and feel rejected. That's life. You did the best you could. You didn't lose anything but a few minutes of your time, and you probably learned something you didn't know before.

What should you do next? Just look for someone else and start flirting. There are millions of guys out there, and there's bound to be one who is just right for you.

BUSINESS BEFORE PLEASURE

Now, what if you're with a man, but you don't get a chance to utilize your femininity and magnetism before he already knows how smart and successful you are? It happens almost every day. It's called a business situation.

You may be sexually attracted to a nice single man with all the right qualities, yet your work depends on your giving him a dazzling display of your intellectual gifts and showing him how efficient and aggressive you are. In short, that you're as good a man as he is or better. (Because, of course, everyone is male at the office.)

You might have to sell him your product or your service, or

he might be a part of a large group to which you have to give a presentation. Well, don't worry about crossed signals here. As long as you're speaking to him as a businesswoman, go for the gold. You won't hurt your chances one bit if you handle both your business and personal situations correctly. Sell him, pitch him, convince him, and do your deal. Then, when it is over and you meet him over the buffet table or in the hallway, *don't* pick up the conversation again. If you do, you're still doing business. Let him reach forward and bring you out. Be a woman again. Wait, give him your most receptive look, and smile. He has already seen your dynamic, powerful side; now, let him see your other side, the shy, soft, sensual one. Trust me, he's looking for it. Be seductive through your eyes and flirtatious with your smile.

A masculine man will be able to respect you as a businesswoman and still cherish your soft feminine side. But you must provide him with chasing space. Let him take control, and speak first!

To sum up then: Choosing to be the female energy means packaging your femininity by being a woman in a desirable body, a lovable, well-cared-for body. Marketing your femininity has to do with going out where men are, picking one, and signaling him that you're receptive and that you are going to respect him when he makes his advance. Whether or not you're going to have to say, "Oh, thank you, but I'm leaving for China in the morning," or if you have to reject him because he's married or turns out not to be as interesting as you thought, he at least has been supported for approaching you. If all women would treat men with respect, then men would find it easier to approach the one woman who will indeed be his special woman. That could be you.

Now, if you do follow these primary rules about being the female in the relationship, you will most likely reap the reward: being asked out by a masculine man. You can even make a few seemingly fatal mistakes in your technique, like talking too much about yourself or criticizing his point of view, and still succeed. But you can never make the ultimate mistake—going home and sleeping with him. Just as there are clear rules for getting a man, there are clear rules for keeping him. The foremost and most formidable is: NO SEX WITHOUT COMMITMENT.

PART THREE

THE FOUR STAGES
OF A RELATIONSHIP

The Perfect Phase
(1–3 months)

CHAPTER 9

Finding Your Prince

You have now reached the point where you know and hopefully understand my concepts for a successful relationship. You have taken the test to determine whether you are more suited to the female or male energy. If you've chosen to be the female, you've learned to flirt with attractive men. If you've chosen to be the male, I hope you've already asked a few men out. Either way, I assume there either is or soon will be someone in your life.

Now, for the first time in your life, you will enter the four stages of a relationship knowing who you are and the kind of man you want. But first, I want to take you through the "Perfect Phase."

This consists of the first three months of a relationship, during which you feel as though you have finally met the one person on earth who is "right" for you. This is the time when the rosy glow of romance colors everything. Everything the two of you do and say is perfect.

But this is not a sexual period, unless you have committed to one another. That would be premature, and treacherous, because as you've learned, feminine women bond through sex, and if you mate too soon, you are likely to be condemning the relationship to a sexual experience rather than to a lovemaking experience. Sex for sex's sake is not fulfilling to someone who wishes to make love. And making love is a combination of physical chemistry, mental compatibility, and emotional generosity.

So it is in this period that you must learn whether you share the three most important ingredients for a successful relationship.

CHEMISTRY, COMPATIBILITY, AND COMMUNICATION

Chemistry is sexual attraction. It is that funny feeling you get in the pit of your stomach when he's in the same room. It's my belief that we live too long these days to be with one person intimately without having chemistry.

Some women rationalize away the need for chemistry if a man is cute or nice, educated and successful. Insecure men sometimes do the same, if the woman is very beautiful and he needs a girlfriend who looks good to other men. But to me, chemistry is a prime ingredient in a marriage-bound relationship.

Compatibility involves harmonious morals and ethics, communication and direction—all of the things that make up a good friendship as well as a loving romantic relationship. But being compatible does not mean that you and he must be clones. On the contrary, it is best if one of you has greater assets in the physical, playful area and the other in the mental, thinking area.

Compatibility also has its nonnegotiable and negotiable aspects, which must be dealt with before sex, because people who have sex too soon tend to think they are compatible even when they are not. They believe that love (sex) is all they need. Then, when the honeymoon period of three months is over, reality hits, and the two people are faced with each other's defects. It is at this point that these couples become bored and often break up.

Communication is of utmost importance. You must talk to him to find out who he really is, beyond your projection of him. If he is a masculine man, he must be able to know what he thinks and wants and ask you how you feel about it. And you must be able to respond with feelings, and not be afraid to say no when you have to. You must both be honest about your hopes and dreams as well as your likes and dislikes.

During this Perfect Phase you will both be on your best behavior, eager to please, especially during all of the traumatic moments that usually come up in the beginning of the relationship—meeting each other's parents or kids or closest friends. We all know that Prince Charming can turn out to be the "wolf," so how do you see beyond his dazzling exterior and really tell if you've met the right guy for you? Sometimes you just have to trust your female—feeling—intuition (or your male—thinking—intuition, if you've chosen to be the male energy), but mostly you have to spend nonsexual time discovering who this man really is.

A man and woman must know what each other's "life goals" are. Often these will come up in conversation as early as the first date, and when he talks, you listen. Find out if he wants to get married, or if he prefers the single life. What about children? You might tell him of your yearning to have them and learn that he is determined never to be a father, or maybe he's already raised one family and doesn't want to start another, no matter how crazy about you he seems.

Ask him about his career goals. He will probably be thrilled that you are interested enough to ask, but only if he believes it's not because you want to know how much money he has. Then, when he tells you about his plans, think about what compromises you might have to make in order for him to attain his goals. For example, if you find out that this terrific man is saving his money to buy an Alaskan shrimp boat, you may have quickly run into a nonnegotiable snag, and the relationship may be better off ending before you get involved and before one or both of you gets hurt.

Remember, if you're a feminine-energy woman, you can't ask a man to change for you. You can only say, "If you are set on living on an Alaskan shrimp boat, then I don't think I should see you anymore, because I want to live in a warm climate."

Of course, he might say, "Well, I wouldn't mind owning a shrimp boat in the Gulf of Mexico." If that's okay with you, your relationship may then be back on track, but only because it was *his* decision. He can change to keep you or to please you, but not because you tell him to.

Investigate your compatibility: Do you like the way he dresses, the way he acts? What about his religion, politics, ethics, financial assets, educational background, and even more practical things such as whether one of you is a morning person and the other one a night person. Learn about his food habits and smoking or drinking habits or addictions. These are real issues for you to explore.

The second question you should ask about a partner before becoming emotionally involved is: *Does he keep his commitments?*

Remember, a feminine woman must protect herself from bonding to a man who is not responsible enough to live up to the commitments he makes.

Carla, a young artist who was a regular at my seminars, was crazy about Val, an actor whom she had been dating about six weeks. In the beginning of their relationship, Val lived up to all of his promises, but as the weeks passed, Carla noticed that Val started to change.

It began one evening when he was late to pick her up for a date. This quickly became a pattern, unless they were going someplace that was especially important to him. Often he failed to call her when he said he would, and one time he even kept her waiting alone in a restaurant for over an hour because he had run into an old friend on the street and had stayed to talk.

Carla told Val how she "felt" about his behavior, and although he said he would change, he didn't. In fact, as time passed, this pattern continued, and regretfully, because she really liked him, she ended the relationship.

But of course not every man is like Val. Many men will live up to their commitments, which will allow the two of you to begin to build a trusting relationship.

Terri, a divorced cosmetics salesperson with two kids, had

been burned badly by her ex-husband. He left her for a younger woman after fifteen years of marriage and never paid the child support she had been awarded in court. Her experiences with other men since she was single did nothing to add to her faith in men.

Then she met Donald, a good-looking, recently divorced businessman, and although she accepted a date with him, she assumed that he would be like all the others.

But Donald never did disappoint. He was a man of his word. He did exactly what he said he'd do and expected her to do the same. When he set a time to pick her up, he was there or called ahead to explain why he would be late. He was great with her children, too, and lived up to all his commitments with them.

After a few weeks they committed to one another and finally made love, and this was one of the best experiences of her life. Terri was still waiting for the joker in the deck, but there was no joker. Donald was a man who lived up to his commitments.

At the end of one year, Terri and Donald married, and they now have a little girl of their own. Meanwhile, he also supports the children from her previous marriage. Terri was lucky to have met a man who lives up to his commitments.

My definition of love is: "THE ONLY WAY YOU KNOW YOU LOVE YOURSELF AND OTHERS IS BY THE COMMITMENTS YOU ARE WILLING TO MAKE AND KEEP."

WHY MEN DON'T CALL BACK

Often a woman will have a great time on the first few dates with a new man. He says he will call soon, then he doesn't, and she can't understand why. We've all been there—and it hurts as much whether you're a teenage girl or a woman executive well into your forties.

The reason is that often when a man is out on a date, his body is there, but his soul is not—which means his mind and his will are elsewhere. And, since most men, as you have learned, have difficulty thinking and feeling at the same time, on the first few dates he's not likely to be thinking about you as a whole person. Rather, what he's mostly feeling is lust, and he's concentrating primarily on getting you into the sack. Later, when he's alone and no longer eyeing your body, he can begin to think about you as a human being. It is then that he may decide that, for whatever reason, you and he are not right for each other.

Sure, it may be that what he really wants is casual sex, and he senses you're not available for that, in which case he has probably done you a favor. But, for whatever reason, once he is alone, he has to distill everything he's learned about you to decide whether or not to call back.

Waiting is hell, but I maintain that a man is not gone unless it has been eight weeks, because it can take that long for him to process a decision.

For four weeks, a man can usually keep himself busy dating, working, and living without you. But if he is really interested, somewhere between six and eight weeks he will begin to miss you, and then he will call.

Can you call him? No, not if you're calling to ask him out. If he left something at your house, sure, you can then call and arrange to have it returned—and to give him the opportunity to ask you out. If you're planning to attend an event that you think he might enjoy, you can ask him to escort you and join a group of people. If you're having a party, you can invite him. But you must not ask him out on a date unless you want to be—you got it, the masculine energy.

Now, here's the good part. Even though you may be designing the wedding gown by the time he drops you off after the first date, as soon as he leaves, you will begin to forget about him. I don't know how many women tell me that they've gotten a call a month after the date from a man whose name they've forgotten. Men can't understand why we are so fickle, and we can't understand why they are so insensitive. And that's the way it is.

So, when you go out on a date, put his name down on a

calendar. If he doesn't call in eight weeks, he doesn't like you. But by that time, you are not likely to care.

PLAYING OUT YOUR ROLE

If he does call back and you begin dating, it is imperative that you play out your chosen role. If he's the male, he leads, and you follow.

If you are a balanced female, you will be an assertive "male" at the office, in an emergency, or when you are alone. But you also must know when to be docile.

"Unbalanced" women either cannot be assertive because they are too "female" and submissive, or they are too "male" and assertive to follow anyone docilely. A balance of both qualities will allow "undependence"—a time to be dependent and a time to be independent.

During this one-to-three-month period, he chooses the places you will go, the restaurants, movies, events you attend together, and he "always" pays. What he is doing is using his finances to court you into understanding the degree of financial security and status he will give you, if and when the two of you get married.

In this phase, he will also be the *experience giver* and the *gift giver* in the relationship. You may reward him later, but always at a lesser level and mostly in abstract ways.

How do you give back in abstract ways? By showing that you respect and trust him. By not correcting his ideas, changing his suggestions, criticizing his opinions, or arguing with his philosophy. By being affectionate and by doing things that, in effect, make him feel good.

As you date him, you continue to magnetize him toward you by looking good, sounding good, smelling good, tasting good, being lovable and responsive, and not "giving" until you receive. You are sweet and kind and say things like "Gee, you're nice," and, "Thanks, so much," and "I appreciate that." It's called *affection*.

If he takes you out a few times, cook him one meal. Make

your gifts less expensive than his. You will know inside your-self whether you owe him (which is good) or he owes you (which is not), or whether you are neutrally equal (which is worse).

Do not neutralize his generous, protective, cherishing gifts by giving equally, or by cherishing his feelings ahead of your own. A masculine man can't fall in love when he receives, only when he gives. It is good for you to feel indebted to your man, because this often generates a feeling of appreciation and re-spect, which allows you to be more available and more recep-tive to him sexually.

BEWARE OF EQUALITY

Equality ruins the romance between a man who craves respect and a woman who wishes to have her feelings cherished. This is especially important during this Perfect Phase, when your primary roles are being established. Later, you can renegoti-ate the male-female roles if you both choose to, but in the beginning, if your new man says, "Why can't you pay half," say something in essence like "You have every right to ask me to split the cost of our dates; however, I am not comfort-able doing that. I respect men who want to protect and cher-ish me. I feel safe and secure with them, which allows me to be more vulnerable and intimate, especially sexually. Do you want this, or do you want to find someone else who agrees with you?"

Some men upon hearing this will leave you quickly in or-der to avoid the responsibilities you require. But others will breathe a sigh of relief: Finally, they have found a woman who likes a man.

When a man *cherishes* you, he will like giving more to you. He will feel secure that you "need" him and will not leave quickly. He will like being your protector. He feels secure in his caretaking ability, and you will feel secure and therefore re-spectful and loving toward him, and he loving toward you.

You must nourish a man's self-esteem. Women who cannot allow themselves to feel "little" next to their man are often afraid to be vulnerable and intimate. They believe they must feel "equal to" or, worse, "better than" their man.

This is human nature: We like to feel empowered. But unless you want to feel this way all the time and be the masculine energy in a relationship, resist such short-term temptations in favor of the higher ground—the long-range objective of a successful relationship with a masculine man.

So for ninety days, you and your new man are dating and relating, and he is giving, you're receiving. He is putting out his best foot, and you're watching to see if he sticks it in his mouth. Although you may be fooling around a little sexually, you are not going all the way. What you *are* doing is communicating by talk and touch. Hopefully, you are both being honest. He is saying what he wants, and you are saying what you don't want.

How do you get your man to keep coming back for more, so you can get through the Perfect Phase to the next, more treacherous Imperfect Phase? By doing just exactly what I have suggested—look good, smell good, taste good, and sound good. Just keep doing it, and he'll keep coming back. It's like an animal in a "humane" trap. He will walk in and walk out, walk in and walk out. The secret is not to close the door against him or after him. Let him capture you on his own terms.

Women have to be patient, and the only way they can do that is to be anchored in their own self-love. Getting a man requires an enormous amount of patience. I often say that good men are like whales. If they're lying on the beach, they're probably sick. A good man is hard to capture, and you can't do anything to capture him—he has to capture you with his own energy.

I often ask the women at my seminars who have chosen to be the feminine energy to take this oath:

"I PROMISE TO SERVE MY OWN WOMANHOOD BY LEADING THE

MAN IN MY LIFE TOWARD A HIGHER LEVEL OF SPIRITUALITY, BY REQUIRING HIM TO LOVE ME BEFORE HE MAKES LOVE TO ME, TO SERVE MY FEELINGS BEFORE HE ASKS ME TO SERVE HIS THINKING, AND TO ALLOW ME TO SET THE SPIRITUAL STANDARD IN OUR SEXUAL AFFAIRS, FOR THE BENEFIT OF US BOTH."

CHAPTER 10

No Sex Without Commitment

(*How Men Fall in Love and Women Fall into Bondage*)

Women who are interested in marriage must *signal* men *before sex* that they are moving toward marriage, or too often the woman will be hurt and time will be wasted. This is the core of my sex training—how to have committed sex.

Not long after you meet, maybe even on the first date, a man will invite you to play the masculine game of "Let's consummate the relationship during the Perfect Phase, when we don't know the downsides of our personalities, but the chemistry is really rolling."

Don't be insulted by an honest request for casual sex. It means his body likes your body, and he wants to do what's natural for bodies to do. Men want to play after work. One of the things that they want to play at is sex. So, be grateful to whoever asks you for sex as long as he does it courteously, and say thank you even when you say no.

If you agree to casual sex, what you are really saying is, "I don't know you, but who cares? Let's do it because our bodies want it, and, hopefully, pretty soon, we'll fall in love and get married, I guess."

Unfortunately, things don't work that way. Monogamy, it

appears, is a "female" situation, while masculine men may be comfortable with multiple sex partners. So how do you know when to have sex with a new man? That's easy. After he gives you a commitment.

A man knows before he meets a woman if he is available for commitment, but often what it takes is a woman requiring him to make that commitment. This means nothing less than a woman saying, "I am not going to have sex with you until you promise me continuity, exclusivity, and longevity," or in other words, commitment.

This is a promise that he must make soberly at least a day in advance of consummation and preferably in the cold light of day when you are talking and not engaging in sexual foreplay. If he will promise that he is interested in a long-term, sexually exclusive, continuous relationship leading to a mutual goal that you both appreciate, which may or may not include a legal marriage, then he is on his way to love.

Continuity—A man must promise that once you have sex with him, you and he will continue to have sex on a regular basis, and that this isn't just a brief fling.

Longevity—Is he looking for a one-night stand or a possible lifetime commitment? Find out what his long-term plans are for relating to a woman—you.

If you want a long-term relationship, then he must be available for, and be willing to have, one with the same goals as yours. If you want marriage and children, he doesn't have to propose marriage, but rather, "I'm available for marriage and children, and if things work out between us, I'm willing."

Monogamy—Since masculine men are naturally very polygamous, you must find out with whom else he is having a sexual relationship. Does he want to continue having sex with his ex-wife or old girlfriend, or with any new ladies he happens to meet? Or are you the only one? This promise is the most decisive of the three aspects of commitment, and the most difficult to extract. Masculine men do not easily give up sexual freedom, so his agreement is a sign that he is on his way to love.

Sometimes a man will make two out of three promises, a two-thirds commitment. If you get continuity and longevity, he's probably having sex with other people. If you get sexual exclusivity and continuity but don't get longevity, you're looking at a short romance. He may not yet be ready for marriage.

If a man is not "intellectually" ready to take on the responsibility of a woman and possibly children, he will say, "Sorry, but I'm really not ready to make that kind of commitment. I just want to have some fun." If he says this, he is telling you candidly that he just wants sex and that he hasn't fallen out of his bachelor attitude.

And if he tells you this, believe me, he means it. Don't think you can seduce a "masculine" man. You can't. He's too smart for that. But usually, instead of believing him, we women translate his words into, "Once he sees how wonderful I am, he'll fall in love with me, and we'll be married." More often than not, it doesn't happen.

When Beverly, a fledgling movie producer, met Bruce, an aspiring film director, at a dinner party one Friday night, they talked about what they wanted in life. Beverly was candid about the fact that she was looking for a man to marry, and Bruce was just as candid when he told her that he was just out of a divorce and probably would not be ready to remarry for a long time. He said he was just interested in playing the field.

Although Beverly heard the words, she was so attracted to Bruce that she invited him back to her apartment. She didn't plan to have sex with him, because she knew it was too soon, but after a few passionate kisses, she got "swept away," and Bruce spent not only the night but the entire weekend with her.

By Sunday morning, as they were reading the newspapers in bed, Beverly began picturing the two of them married and living a perfect life. She did this right up until the moment on Sunday afternoon when Bruce gave her his card and left to go to the airport and pick up another woman, whom, he admitted to Beverly, he had been sleeping with for nearly six months, and who had been away for the weekend.

FRIENDSHIP IS THE ROOT, SEX IS THE BLOOM

Theoretically, I believe that a couple should wait until they are into the Imperfect Phase and can see one another as whole people—imperfections and all—before they consummate their relationship. Compatibility, along with natural chemistry and good communication skills, is the "friendship quotient" in a relationship. When a woman *feels* her man is a dear friend before making love, she is safer in her choice. It is not enough for a man and woman to have good sex together, they must also feel safe as friends together. Talking things out before sex allows both people to be grounded in human values.

I advise women to talk about all the issues that are of significant interest to them and to their man. If you have strong feelings about politics, religion, ethics, hobbies, cultural events, sports, size of family, career goals, physical defects that might impact on the relationship, past marriages and why they failed, you should talk about them before sex. However, I warn you—don't discuss old boyfriends or past sexual experiences. A man likes to idealize his woman, and it is not in your best interest to appear "shopworn."

A man is not trying to hurt you by getting you to give sex to him. A polygamous married man may take good care of both his mistress and his wife, but it is usually the wife to whom he is "committed." She is the one he is "in love with," physically, mentally, and emotionally. His mistress is his "lust mate." Men marry from their brains to their bodies and women from their bodies to their brains.

Men who want sex only decide *not* to be responsible for their woman's feelings. They hold her responsible for herself, so if she gives sex without commitment, it is her loss and his gain. Masculine men believe that if a woman is "man" enough to have casual sex, he has no responsibility to deal with birth control or the possibility of disease. Every "man" for himself, even if one of them is a "woman."

A woman who is attracted to a man is much better off if she waits for sex until she hears a good deal for her life. Remember, talk before touching. Usually, good communication and open sharing on significant issues will build a foundation based on reality. Ask yourself these questions. Do I "like" this person as a human being? Could he and I be real friends, or is he primarily a sex object for me?

I like to tell women to seek out the "puzzle" and the "gem" within the man. The puzzle is, "What makes this person tick? Do I like it?" The gem is, "What is this person's gift? Humor? Honesty? Intelligence?"

The best way to avoid a painful surprise is not to act sexually on your imagination and your projection of his perfection. Find out who he really is. Pathological liars can fabricate perfect stories that will seduce some of you into a bad relationship. If you are insecure about believing him for whatever reason, take him to a third party for a talk about goals and objectives before sex. This person could be a friend, a member of your family whose judgment you trust, or a respected religious leader. If you have enough money to spend an hour or two with a professional counselor/therapist, do it. You are worthy of protection from the danger and agony of a bad sexual experience.

Ultimately, however, life is a series of risks. You do your footwork, make your decision, and then see the results. The "rats" and "con men" are out there. If you get into a bad deal, get help as soon as you can in order not to become soured on love and life.

OXYTOCIN, THE LOVE HORMONE

Why do feminine-energy women have to get a commitment before they have sex with a man? Because feminine women bond through sex, but masculine men do not.

Most liberated, sexually active women, like Leslie (who slept with Mark the first night they met), believe they can maintain self-centered control over their emotions after sex. What they don't realize is that casual, noncontracted sex in a normal woman triggers a bonding that verges on physical addiction. This is due to a sexually stimulated hormone called oxytocin, which is predominant in females and which triggers orgasm. Soon the sound of his voice, the look on his face, the touch of his hands, even the smell of his cologne, become intensely associated with the addictive pleasure that oxytocin brings, and keeps "her" bonded to "him," even after they separate.

You know the story: On the first date, he was passable. On the second, he was okay. Then you had *great sex*! And now you can't stand the thought of him ever leaving your side. Your body tells you you're in love—even though your brain is saying he's all wrong for you. What's going on? It's not love—it's *oxytocin*.

Even worse, according to Marie Carmichael, Ph.D., at Stanford University, is that women who are sexually aroused by the taste, touch, sight, smell, and sound of a man can love that man addictively, while the man remains physically noncommitted.

Chemistry told Leslie she was with the right man and that she should act on this. Compatibility was something she believed she could manipulate by being whatever Mark wanted her to be. She twisted herself into someone who put his needs, wants, and feelings ahead of hers, thinking that when she really needed his support, he would be a loving reciprocator. But Mark was still entrenched in his childhood view of women who, like his mother, give and give, with little need to receive.

As for communication, Leslie began body-to-body touching and left talking for later. But, when later came, it was too late to say, "We are really not compatible, we don't fit together after all," because she was strongly bonded to Mark, and she suffered addictive symptoms when he began to pull away. She found herself begging him and chasing him. Mark, on the other hand, could walk away and be with another woman with small effort.

It took over a year of Leslie's time and a total separation from Mark's body for her oxytocin rush to subside and the bonding to melt. It can take up to two years to break this kind of addiction, so I strongly suggest that for physical, mental, and emotional well-being, you be very careful whom you "let in" to your body, and under what conditions. If you haven't negotiated a commitment before you make love, you're probably not going to afterward. Left-lobe-oriented masculine men do not bond through sex. They bond through the commitments they make and keep.

When I talk about commitment, I am really talking about choice. And that choice might be a one-night stand, a weekend affair, a summer love, or even a relationship with a married man. But at least you know where you stand before you risk becoming bonded.

Requiring a man to commit to you before having sex with him does not mean you are bound to him for life, nor he to you. Instead, you both are entering into an honest and mutual good-faith contract in which either one of you may decide that you're not destined to be life mates—in which case, no hard feelings, only natural human sadness that a dream has died. Life is often painful, but it need not be hurtful. We determine our reactions to pain. Healthy men and women handle life's broken dreams without hurting themselves or others. Time heals all wounds when you remain rational and balanced.

WHY MASCULINE MEN DO NOT BOND THE WAY THAT FEMININE WOMEN DO

Why don't masculine men get "hooked" on sex and bond the way women do? Because bonding is an experience that is created by the receiving of physical pleasure, and although oxytocin works the same way in men as in women, women seem to be more susceptible to its emotional effects. It has been found that during sex, women produce higher levels of oxytocin than men do, and that it takes more oxytocin for women to achieve orgasm than it takes men, which also impacts on the addiction.

Another reason that assertive, dynamic men don't "bond" to the physical is because they override their feminine aspects and their feelings with logical, testosterone-based, action-oriented behavior. They are after good sex at the cheapest price. Being in control of the deal and competitive with their peers for the prize (you) is the fun of a good masculine man.

By the way, there are men who do bond through sex. They are predominately "feminine" men who are more right-lobe, feeling-oriented; older men whose testosterone is diminishing; left-handed men who have more access to their feelings neurologically; and men who have been raised predominantly by women and who have learned about feeling-centered living from them.

HOW MEN FALL IN LOVE AND HOW WOMEN SHARE LOVE

Only a masculine man falls in love; a feminine woman doesn't. She must already be in love with herself. If a woman has been well loved by her father, she will be in love with herself. Then, when a man proposes to her, she will be able to consider how and what he can *add* to her life. If she can do better by herself, she will say, "No, thank you." But if he can add to her life, she simply shares the love she has for herself with him. And he will make her life better for the sharing.

A man cannot fall in love with a woman who is not already in love with herself. A woman who loves a man better than herself risks an addictive obsession in which she loses herself completely in service of his narcissistic ego. This is, classically speaking, the woman who will do anything for a man.

Sally worshipped Larry. She loved doing things for him, cleaning his apartment, running errands, and she never complained about his erratic way of making and breaking social commitments. The trouble was, Sally got nothing back.

So many women I see want to marry but *act* as though they want only to be instantly gratified. Men are confused by the crossed message: "Does she want me only to make her body happy? Or does she want me to get to know her first in order to decide if I can marry her?"

A man projects a virtuous image on the woman he wants to marry. When a woman falls from grace and gives a man casual sex, that man can no longer marry her. If I can get it cheap, other men will too, is the way men think.

In the old days, our churches, our parents, and the rest of society ordered women to be virtuous, but when women got the Pill, we rebelled. Our rebelliousness was appropriate, but not our loss of virtue, which turns men *away* from marriage. Men want to be married to women they can predict will not have sex with other men.

The reason men fall in love with the ideal part of a woman is because they have a natural craving to raise their own spiritual standard. When a man falls in love, he is wishing and striving to be a better man. You hear the phrase "A man is a man until he meets a lady, then he becomes a gentleman." The lady sets a standard that requires—but does not demand—him to become a gentleman, and to cherish her.

A boy's rite of passage into manhood is when he stops seeing women, children, and animals as sources of personal gratification and instead sees them as recipients of his manful, loving bounty.

So, if you still think you can get a man to fall in love with you by giving him casual sex, or buying him presents or doing his laundry, think twice! All you'll get is an irresponsible playmate until he meets the lady he falls in love with. And she is the one who will say, "No way, José. Commitment first, before sex."

It is a woman's responsibility to raise a man's level of consciousness from the concrete level of money and sex, where he's comfortable, to the spiritual level of love and relationships, where she's comfortable. If a woman does this correctly, men will usually comply, because they are very logical thinkers. Whether they admit it or not, men want women to set the spiritual standard in the relationship. They already know how to get "laid," and they know that a relationship is only partly about sex. A relationship is about getting bonded, falling in love, and becoming a united team. Men who want to marry *will* wait for committed sex.

A man cannot fall in love with a woman because she is sexy,

rich, a good executive, or a good housekeeper. He can only fall in love with her level of virtue, that part of her that can say no to casual sex, no to loans, and no to moving in without engagement.

Even when a woman is ready to negotiate a commitment, she often finds that she is ready before her man is. A good man is hard to capture, and women have to be patient. The only way they can do that is to be anchored in their own self-love.

Men are a lot slower than we are. By the end of the first date, we're already designing the gown, and they're trying to get our name right. We can go from *A* to *Z* while men think from *A* to *B*.

When a masculine man does surrender and marries, he puts up his money and status and takes on the responsibility not only of his woman, but of everybody she loves. Remember, a good beginning almost always guarantees a good ending.

HOW TO REQUIRE A COMMITMENT AND NOT DEMAND ONE

A feminine woman must *require*, not demand, a commitment from a masculine man, because to demand is masculine, and masculine men do not respond in a positive way to a demand. So how do you "require" a commitment? By waiting until a man asks you for sex, then stating your negative feelings about casual sex. Say something like "Thank you for the compliment. I like being seen by you as sexually desirable. However, I know that I will pleasurably bond to you because I am chemically attracted to you, and I don't know if it is safe yet."

Now you have thanked him, told him you're interested, and said no until talking occurs.

He says, "What would make you feel safe?"

You say, "I would like to know about your goals for us, about other love interests you may have, and about your ability to see me regularly. I am willing to begin a committed, long-term relationship that hopefully could be headed for marriage. Are you?"

Now you have shown him that you are a vulnerable, sensitive woman who loves herself better than she loves him, and he now knows you will not have casual sex, *but* with discussion of longevity, continuity, and exclusivity factors, and with an understanding reached, *might* make love to him.

He then may say to himself, "This woman costs too much for me," and go off to the next girl who is willing to give him a better deal. Or, he may say, "Why didn't she go for it? I'm a good deal."

If he says that, he'll drop his anchor just a bit and take you out again. You still won't sleep with him, but now he's starting to get to know you and like you. If he drops his anchor a bit more and more, this man is "falling in love."

For a man, falling in love is really dangerous. When he does this, he puts his mind, body, heart, soul, and money into the commitment. A man doesn't usually risk falling in love more than once in his life, because when he falls totally in love, he risks his life and his career. And if his relationship fails, he could lose confidence in himself in all facets of his life, including business. He will then usually distrust women to such a degree that he will swear never to fall in love again. This kind of a man uses women for gratification.

So, while it may be in a man's best interest to find a woman who will give him casual sex, it is not in yours, unless you're "man enough" to "get laid," which is far different from making love. "Making love" is based on the feminine principle of a relationship; the relationship is built on friendship and expressed through sex. "Getting laid" is based on the masculine principle of sharing sexual gratification with a friendly partner.

A sensitive woman whose goal is a committed relationship is usually intuitively aware of the possible mistake of "going all the way" with a man whose agenda is unknown to her, and she will be reluctant to have casual sex without knowing why she feels that way. If she overrides her natural apprehension and "goes for it," she soon finds herself in the pain of a relationship that is not fulfilling.

Instead of having sex, try going dancing, getting a massage, and starting an exercise program!

Judy, an interior designer, came to one of my seminars and admitted that she had a history of casual sexual relationships and lots of pain, but she was determined to stop.

When she met Tod, a handsome and successful doctor, on a blind date her friends had arranged, there was lots of chemistry between them. As the evening progressed, they also found out how much they had in common. They were of the same religion, had a similar socioeconomic background, liked the same movies and books, and laughed at the same jokes. The only thing they didn't share, Judy found out at the end of the evening, was their view on monogamy. Tod admitted honestly that although he wanted to sleep with her, he had no intention of settling down with her or any other woman, for the next few years anyway. Judy chose to decline Tod's invitation to "bed." Instead, she became friends with him and kept herself clean in mind and body, clear to meet a man who did want a commitment, which, eventually, she did.

WHEN SAYING "NO" IS PAINFUL

When Cathy, a creative and talented magazine writer, was introduced by a friend to Neal, an attractive surgeon, there was an immediate chemical spark, and to Cathy's delight, Neal soon shared the fact that he was looking for a committed relationship with the right person.

However, Neal pressured Cathy for sex after their second date, and even though her attraction to him made her "feel" like melting into his arms, she told him how she felt about "casual sex" and what it would take for her to "make love."

Neal candidly told Cathy that it was unthinkable for him to commit to her without knowing how compatible they were sexually. He said that for him the spontaneity of good sex with the "right" woman brought on the commitment, that although he liked her very much, he found her "requirements" too calculating for his taste.

The next day Cathy was full of self-doubt, afraid that Neal would not call her again. Even though she knew she would firmly hold to her requirements, she told me how painful it was to say no.

I helped her to realize that the loss of a man who leaves when you say no to casual sex or to other requests for you to "perform" can be painful but not hurtful. What is hurtful is for a woman to give of herself totally and find out that it is still not enough.

Relationships cost. Casual dates and sex cost less pragmatically but do not achieve the committed intimacy we *may* want in our lives. They can be costly emotionally to the woman who becomes bonded.

It is not the orgasm itself, but the *intent* (commitment) behind the orgasm that counts. Making love is "satisfying" in a totally encompassing way when two people decide to commit because they *add* to their already existing human friendship the aspect of sexual fulfillment. But when the intent is only to "fulfill or gratify" physical needs as a priority *before* a commitment, a tone is set that is *not* romantic.

The truth is that romance is anticipation. Romance is between the ears, not between the legs. Romance is courtship, not dating. Romance is making love, not having sex. Romance is a commitment, an act of will between two people.

It is easy to find a "sex" partner. But it is my intent to assist you in making love with someone who wants to make love to *you* and who is willing to commit to the process before being gratified.

Making love requires an ability and willingness to be intimate. In order to build intimacy, you must verbally communicate your wants and feelings. You must learn to communicate and negotiate, or you will set in motion the manipulations and games that will ultimately destroy what you have together.

I believe that by asking Cathy, who wants to be the "female energy" in a relationship, to stop being generous, protective, and cherishing of a man, even if it means "losing" him, I am offering her a second chance. When she said no to casual sex with Neal, who was a masculine man, *he* then had two choices. He could either sell out to have casual sex with a masculine woman, or he could choose to investigate another path with Cathy, the way to intimacy and commitment.

If Neal chose to sell out, Cathy would be none the worse.

HOW MEN TEST WOMEN

Like Neal, many masculine men test the women they are attracted to by seeing if they will "mother" them physically. What they really need is to meet a woman who will not love them like a "giving" mother but will like them as a self-centered, receiving female, until both parties want sex as a means of bonding and lovemaking and will forsake all other relationships.

A man is a man. He is a polygamous animal one minute and a human being the next. He must be *required* to blend both of these aspects by a woman who is so confident and in sync with herself that she will refuse him sex until she can be certain of his commitment. For it is that sense of security and safety that allows her to surrender to the man who shows her he wants her so much that he is willing to voluntarily give up his drive to have sexual relations with many women.

Of course a man will attempt to con, cajole, and undermine you when you say no to casual sex. His "head" tells him that he should not be doing this, but his "nature" challenges him to push past your resistance to "get his needs met."

Lust attracts us to someone we may like and ultimately love, but when a man settles for lust alone, he *eliminates* liking and love. He knows deep inside that the woman he can get into bed with only a little push cannot be trusted as a virtuous ideal woman to marry and grow old with. He knows that her sense of self-worth is so shaky that she can be easily manipulated and used, which in turn causes him to feel disgust or guilt; or he knows she is attempting to control him through seductive giving.

Neither way works.

A woman who has "given" sex only to find that it has made little difference in a man's way of relating to her often feels used and abused and suffers the anger of man-hating. The way to avoid feeling confused and damaged is to say *no* to casual sex, unless that is all you want.

WHEN YOU'VE SAID NO TO CASUAL SEX, AND HE'S NOT CALLING BACK

If you have said no to casual sex to a man you like, and if you choose to be the feminine energy, you must bite the bullet and wait eight weeks for him to call you.

Remember, a normal, right-handed, focused, logical man needs four to eight weeks to evaluate the loss of you. This is a decision of emotional significance involving both left-lobed logic, in this case: "Do I want her enough to call her again?" and right-lobed feelings: "I miss her. She is really a nice, sexy lady. Should I call again?"

If he calls in two to four weeks, it means he was ready for a commitment and needed only to evaluate things a little while. Many men can manage four weeks apart from a woman they care about quite easily. If he calls after six weeks, which is a crucial time, he has made a rational, male decision. As I said before, eight weeks is critical. If he hasn't called within that time frame, stop waiting and go on to other men and other experiences.

So, what happened to Neal and Cathy?

As time passes, a man like Neal who is not accustomed to being turned down by a woman who is obviously sexually attracted to him must handle certain questions:

Q. "Why was Cathy different from the others?"
A. "Because she is virtuous, not needy."

Q. "Could I have done something better to 'conquer' her?"
A. "Maybe. Perhaps I'll try again."

Q. "What should I make of my 'failure to succeed'?"

A. "Discount her. She is nothing to me. Others are easier and better."

                        Or

"Become irritated thinking about her and want resolution."

                        Or

"Call her back in six to eight weeks to try again."

                        Or

"I realize that Cathy is a good woman and that I will have to surrender and agree to a commitment to get her for myself."

If Neal called and asked to see her, he would be signaling that the "courtship" was on and the dating over. In any case, Neal would almost surely remember Cathy as the one woman who loved herself enough to "qualify the buyer"—and at some deep level, he will appreciate her virtue.

I have found that men *do* feel guilty about casual sex relationships, but for them it is a little like eating potato chips—you can't stop with one. Sexual addiction *is* a problem for men in a world of generous women who manipulate with sex and money to "buy" a man's love (lust).

THE SHARK CAGE

As it turned out, while Cathy was waiting out her "eight weeks," she learned that Neal was having sex with two other women. She realized that had she said yes to him, she would have been just another woman in his harem.

But Cathy was confused. What kind of man was Neal, anyway? He had seemed so nice and sincere. Now she wondered: If he indeed called her back, should she go out with him?

I told Cathy that Neal was just a normal "male" who withheld data about his private life because he had no obligation to divulge information that would all but eliminate his success with her. The truth was that Neal was tired of some of the other women in his "harem" and wanted a new one. He talked of wanting an intimate, permanent relationship, but he went about getting it in a nonintimate way, that is, genitals first, heart second.

Men play on women's fantasies that "he" loves the same way "she" loves. *He does not!* Many women act as though it were a man's responsibility to help a woman be a woman. But a man's nature dictates that he get his needs met. If a woman wants to "give in" to him, why shouldn't he accept?

If we ask *beforehand*, we may find out about his "other women" and take care of ourselves. If we don't ask beforehand, he will *not offer information.* Why should he?

I often say that masculine men are like sharks, and we must remember that sharks never sleep. They are always moving, looking for their next prey. Little girls must be taught not to go into the water and play with them. Even good divers do not go down unprotected. They use shark cages. You need a shark cage too.

You can't trap a shark unless he is sedated. He smells the cage and runs away. At least with my system, we show the cage to the shark up front and invite him in.

By the way, Cathy and Neal's story hasn't ended. Six weeks after he walked out of her apartment, Neal did call her and ask for a date, thereby beginning their "courtship" period, which consisted of their getting to know each other without sex until he felt "safe" enough with Cathy to give up his "harem" and commit.

THE DIFFERENCE BETWEEN COURTING AND DATING

For a man, there is a difference between "courting" and "dating." When he is courting, he has a mind-set to mate, to be committed to a long-term, monogamous relationship that may or may not include marriage.

In his mind, courting means he has spotted a woman whom he intuitively knows could be his lover, his wife, and the mother of his children. He is going to win her over with his magnificence like any proud peacock. He is ready to commit before he meets her. When he sees her, he is first drawn to her outward beauty, which looks right to him. He then begins to pursue her with dates, phone calls, and small gestures of affection like flowers, cards, and gifts. Often he does not try to get her into bed too quickly, out of deference to her supposed higher morality. He is patient and takes the time to "do it right."

A woman makes a big mistake if, upon dating a man who is slow to make a sexual advance, she asks him if he is gay or becomes the sexual aggressor. Either of these approaches can lead to sex based on *her* request, which often turns a man off for the long term, *or* can result in a termination of his romantic, idealized courtship. Aggressive sexual behavior on the part of the woman may produce a purely sexual relationship or may even end the relationship. This is because as soon as sex begins, a form of possessiveness begins, based on your mutual minimal knowledge of the other person's true personality.

I know it is hard to wait, especially when the physical attraction is strong and you've played everything up to this point by my rules, but you must wait.

Ann, a blond conservative executive secretary, was looking for a committed relationship but was having no luck until she came to my seminars, learned how to flirt and to package and market her femininity, and duty-dated as per my instructions. Then she met Greg, a quiet, gentle owner of a bookstore.

The first two months of their Perfect Phase went well, but soon Ann became bored with Greg's slow ways. He took months to sexually approach her. Still, at my urging, Ann bided her time and did not ask for more affection, love, or sex. Eventually, they did go to bed together but did not have intercourse, because Greg would not give the entrance fee: longevity, continuity, and exclusivity.

For months, Ann and Greg slept together without sex a few times a week. He asked her to meet his family, who lived out of state, and she passed muster with his powerful mom and his gentle dad and brother. Soon after this trip, Greg proposed marriage, and they had sex. Eventually, Ann's patience paid off. Today she and Greg are happily married and the parents of a baby girl.

Greg wanted to "mate" and took his time finding the right person. But while there are many more men like him out there whose mind-set is to *court* and not *date*, the problem for most women lies in the fact that, from the outside, both the "courting man" and the "dating man" act in the same way. He says what needs to be said to convince you that he is going where you are going—usually toward commitment and marriage.

If a man is lying, you will know it in a matter of *days*, because he will feel guilty using you, and he will make his real intentions clear. So you will not have lost too much time or energy or gotten too bonded sexually.

Psychopaths and criminals can use and abuse for a longer period than normal men, but eventually your intuition will flag you, and you get out, probably with a wounded ego and much less money.

IF YOU'RE ALREADY HAVING CASUAL SEX

So you have already let him "in," and now you're reading this book and realizing that you made a mistake. What do you do? First, cross those pretty long legs of yours and tell him that you are going to stop having sex with him until he's agreed to a commitment.

Say, "I made a mistake. I let our relationship down by giving you casual sex. I'm not going to do that anymore. I understand that you may leave, but from now on, I need longevity, continuity, and exclusivity from you, or that's it."

You are saying those words because you mean them and because you want a man who wants the same things you do. Anything less is no longer acceptable.

During a workshop in Los Angeles, Jennifer, an attorney, came down to the front of the room and revealed that she was in a relationship with Michael, a successful businessman, and that everything was great except for one thing: Her man would not commit to a permanent arrangement toward marriage and children. What to do? I told her flatly, "It's simple. Pull the plug! No more sex! You'll find out soon enough what his intentions are."

Jennifer followed my advice and told Michael that she had made a mistake and would no longer be having sex with him without a commitment. With my system, men usually leave quickly or they stay around for a long time, and my success rate of couples who stay together is very high, partly because they both have a clear understanding of what is expected of them before they get bonded.

Luckily, Jennifer found out that her man did love her and was ready for a commitment. About a month later, she returned to the workshop with Michael, her engagement ring, and a wedding date.

However, not every woman who says no gets as quick or as satisfying a response as Jennifer did.

Lisa, a television executive who came to one of my seminars, confided, "My boyfriend, Edward, and I, after seeing each other steadily for six months, have been fighting a lot lately over commitment. I know that if I don't have sex with him, he'll want to date other women. He says we can be friends, and maybe it will work out later. What should I do?"

I told Lisa that this friendship her boyfriend wants is contact without romance, and that she must say *no*, because seeing him, even on a "friendly" basis, keeps the connection going. For her part, seeing him, even hearing his voice on an answering machine, keeps her bonded. On his part, he gets to use her and other women and keep her available *should* he want her. I told her that it would be too painful to date him while he is having sex with others and that she shouldn't do it.

Often, after you tell a man your requirements, he will hear what you say and walk out the door, and the pain will be intense. You may be unable to eat, or you will overeat. You will talk, cry, and scream. But there is nothing for you to do except *wait eight weeks*.

Marilyn, a nursery-school teacher, had been dating Leon,

her architect boyfriend, for six years. Although they lived in separate apartments, they hardly spent a night without each other. Marilyn was ready to get married, but Leon wanted to keep the status quo.

One day Marilyn decided that enough was enough. Either we get married, she thought, or we're done. She told Leon that evening, and he did as she expected. He said, "You're right, Marilyn. I'm not ready to get married yet, and I don't want to keep you from your goal."

The parting was tearful and tender, and both believed their long relationship was over. Marilyn knew that she was doing what she had to do for herself, although the pain was terrible.

As the weeks passed, although it was not easy, Marilyn went about her life, trying to make new connections and fill the space their relationship left. She thought about Leon a lot but began dating other men. Then, to her surprise, exactly eight weeks after the breakup, he called.

"I made a mistake," he said. "I can't replace you, and I don't want to live without you. Will you marry me?"

Marilyn was stunned. She *never* expected that call, but she was thrilled to get it. She accepted Leon's proposal. They have been happily married now for ten years and are the proud parents of two children.

Marilyn's story is not unusual. Many masculine, bullheaded men must feel the pain of loss before they realize that they want to be married.

EIGHT WEEKS AGAIN

I must emphasize that this is a critical time, when one incorrect action on your part can extend your painful bond to the wrong man. So it is imperative that you understand what is happening during this process.

As I have said, it takes approximately eight weeks for a man to process a decision. For four weeks, he can usually function at least superficially, dating, working, and living. At first his left-lobed logic says, "Who needs her? I'll decide how things go between us. No woman controls me!"

If he is in love with you, and not just using you for sex, but didn't "know" he was in love, somewhere around six to eight weeks he will miss you so badly he may call and ask to be "friends."

Don't do it! This rekindles your oxytocin bonding. Don't listen to his voice on his telephone message recorder or on yours. Change the voice on your recording. Have someone else do your message so he can't get a voice fix off you and be able to stay away longer. Don't taste, touch, smell, see, or hear him, or you will lose that tension-building separation anxiety. Let the rubber band stretch and stretch.

Don't call him for any reason. If you are as patient as Job, you can control your impulsive need to reconnect before eight weeks. If you call him, you lose and he wins. Sex is all you get. And you learn to hate each other.

But if you don't call, as his right lobe *feels* the pain he will realize why he hurts. He misses you. No one else can replace you. He must have another chance to be with you, which will lead him to call you and admit that he is in love with you and wants a commitment.

However, if he does not call in eight weeks, *it's over*. Start duty-dating, dress up, get out, and read self-help books, get on with your life as a single woman. If you have had a long-term relationship, it might take as long as two years to get over him, so don't sit around. A new love will take you away from him.

DON'T GIVE UP

Don't give up on relationships, even if you have an unsuccessful or painful experience. Read this book carefully and learn how to have a successful committed relationship. Then do it, step by step.

Giving up on love is what many men have done, so they settle for casual sex. Instead, evaluate your objectives, maintain your integrity, your physical well-being, and your emotional balance. Remember, whenever you are tempted to give a man sex before he gives you a commitment:

"I PROMISE NEVER TO LOVE A MAN MORE THAN MYSELF, FOR MY SPIRITUAL SAKE AS WELL AS HIS."

WHY SHOULD HE COMMIT?

These days, women claim that men are noncommittal. I claim that women are, and allow men to follow suit. Why should a masculine man restrict his bachelor nature to be responsible for an independent woman and her kids? He would rather invest the money in his life, fun, and property, as long as he can get sex with minimal cost. Self-gratifying, self-centered men are dating self-satisfied, selfless women who like playing and dating as much as they do.

Many men feel castrated and no longer act like "men," fighting and competing for the best sex partner. They have few challenges other than watching sports events and clawing their way up the corporate ladder, which is currently infiltrated by many women *more male* than they are.

They have been put in suits with leftover nooses (ties), stuck in cars for hours each day to struggle to an office often dominated by a woman so hard and tough she would scare the "night-stalker." Then, after work, the poor guy is asked to make love to the fair maiden and marry her so he can work for her and the kids when she won't even respect him enough to let him lead, because she has to be "liberated from the domination of men."

This is not a pretty picture, and it is one that has turned many men toward an uncommitted life or workaholism. Balance must come back to a fair trade of respect for cherishing, by respectful men and by women who wish to be cherished. Let's teach women how to be cherished by first teaching them to cherish themselves.

In the past, men felt a moral obligation to marry. These days, men "respect" a woman's ability to take care of herself and be independent. They see women as "equal" to casual sex the way they are; therefore, they feel no need to protect us, even from themselves.

Only when men get hungry for the best women will they make a deal and settle down. It is the woman's job to set the parameters for the deal. If we say yes to casual sex, we have assumed responsibility for the results. It is our ability to say *No sex without commitment* that is the essence of this book.

CHAPTER 11

How to Get What You Need from a Man Without Ever Asking for It

Learn how to talk to your man. You have only three lessons to learn. They are

1. How to ask for what you want
2. How to say no to what you don't want, without becoming emotional
3. How to negotiate with the man in your life so you can hear what he wants (and doesn't want)

When problems arise in communication, all negotiations and intimacy fail and give way to intimidation and seduction. While these do work, they are based on the fear, sense of guilt, and shame of the victim. Power plays and games take over when negotiation and intimacy are overridden.

In every verbal communication in an intimate relationship, there must be one respected leader and one cherished follower. The respected leader says, "I think and I want" and also asks, "How do you feel?" and then listens. The "female" listens to the thinking and the wanting of the "male," shares positive and negative feelings, and says yes or no. Men who know what they want will not get rejected as often as men who don't, whose ambivalence makes them appear weak and indecisive. Feminine women turn off to men who do not act like respectable leaders.

If you want to be the female energy, and your man does not have the courage to lead but instead asks you what you want and what you think, decline gracefully, and say, "I will tell you what I feel about what you think and want, but I'm uncomfortable leading."

He may accept or rebel. If he rebels and wants you to be the masculine principle, then he must respect your leadership and not just ask you to stick your neck out.

Of course, masculine-energized women *do* know what they want, and their assertiveness is fine, provided it is directed romantically at feminine-energized men who often *don't* know what they want. But be certain to make clear to him that you cherish his feelings. Don't intimidate him into submissiveness.

HOW TO ASK FOR WHAT YOU WANT

If you choose to be the "feminine" energy, you get what you want by *not* directly asking for it, because a direct request may feel like a demand or an order to a masculine man, even if you don't mean it that way. Masculine men can hear an opportunity to please a woman, but they resist women who seem to issue commands. Masculine men pride themselves on their freedom to act, to choose, and to control their own destinies. They enjoy giving to feminine women and making them happy as long as this is not assumed, expected, or demanded.

Most men, when told what you want or think (outside of a work environment), will, instead of obediently giving you what you want, have a "man-to-man" competitive reaction, responding with what *they* want, thus ruining the objective of simply having fun together.

When Marie, a pediatric intern resident at a large hospital, wanted to see her boyfriend, Pete, a surgical intern at the same hospital, to ask him about his free time, she would run up to the floor on which he was working. Pete was so busy that he often enjoyed her pursuing him, but their problems came when he did not want to see her, even when he was free. Sometimes Pete just wanted to be alone or with his friends. When he would tell her this, Marie would try to argue him out of it. Sometimes Pete gave in, but at other times her pushing made him angry and annoyed.

Pete was exhausted from the long hours he worked, and although he tried to explain his point of view to Marie, her emotionalism would overwhelm him, and he would give in to her demands. This went on for about six months until Pete took a stand and threatened to end the relationship if Marie didn't change.

Marie came to one of my seminars along with some other female interns who had heard about my system and how it worked. When she came up onstage, Marie was totally confused about how she had contributed to Pete's dissatisfaction with their relationship.

Although Pete had allowed her to intimidate him simply because it was "easier" for him to do so, she saw it as a "win" for her side. However, I showed her why arguing with Pete had eventually caused the rupture and very nearly brought on the loss of the man she loved.

Through working with me, Marie learned that the only way a relationship as equally balanced as hers and Pete's was could be a success was to choose, by mutual agreement, whose thinking was ultimately respected first. If Marie wanted to be the feminine woman to Pete's masculine man, she needed to understand that even though they were totally equal in education, social skills, and economics, she still needed to defer to him, as long as what he asked of her was ethical and moral.

I taught Marie that she should not push for what she wanted in a logical or "direct" manner. Pete had given Marie permission to pursue him, but that did not mean she could control him. Marie decided that she would be happy respecting Pete's thinking ahead of her own. Marie learned to follow his lead, as long as he cherished her feelings. Marie didn't need to be happy when he said *no* to her requests, but she did need to treat him did need to treat him in a respectful manner. And Pete didn't need to be insensitive to her pain when he turned her down. He needed to cherish her.

Marie learned to ask, "Pete, I know you are busy. Do you want to see me tonight?"

Pete learned to respond in the following way when he didn't want to see her: "Marie, you know I care about you and want to spend time with you, but I don't have a lot of time. I want to be with the guys tonight for a few hours. How do you feel about my saying no?"

Marie's feminine response to this turndown could be, "Pete, I appreciate your time constraint and your wanting to see the guys. Of course I'm not happy about it, but I do not want to hassle you. Have fun." This was an intimate direct transaction in which both people felt respected and cherished, even when pain was involved.

Women attending my lectures and hearing this for the first time often respond with anger. As liberated women, they pride themselves on taking responsibility for their lives and for asserting themselves. What I recommend often seems to be in direct contradiction with self-awareness skills they have come to learn and prize.

And I can almost hear you saying, "Why do I have to put men on an intellectual pedestal? I'm as smart and talented and educated and successful as they are."

The reason is that if you want your man to put you on an emotional pedestal (in a cherishing place), then you do have to put him on an intellectual one (a place of respect). You must not try to teach him, criticize him, belittle him, or compete with him for sexual control. A truly feminine woman shares with her man her feelings about what pleases or does not please her, which allows him to solve a problem—in his way, not hers. She can always reject him if he is not satisfying her, but until she does reject him, she accepts him as "enough," and she does not hurt his feelings by being blunt and tactless.

When I say put your chosen man on an intellectual pedestal, it is with this caveat: as long as you can give him feedback about your feelings concerning his ideas, thoughts, opinions, and beliefs, and he listens with empathy and does not impose immoral or unethical values on you.

The idea is that the female energy automatically gives respect for the male's right to speak. She does not compete or contradict or confront him with her ideas.

Donna, an interior decorator, had been seeing Richard, a computer programmer, for about five months. She'd read that Rod Stewart would be performing live in their town, and she wanted Richard to take her to see him, a simple enough request, except that in the past, whenever she had been assertive and direct in her communication with Richard, he would get annoyed with her. Eventually, though, he would come around.

When this first started happening, Donna was confused. She wondered if Richard was just stingy and resented having to spend his money on her, but then she remembered all the nice things he did for her and gave her, and she knew that was not the problem. It wasn't until she began attending my seminars that she learned what was going wrong in her communication with Richard.

What Donna was doing, in effect, was asking Richard for more or better time together. As I have said previously, this can turn a man into a little boy or a passive-aggressive male who will not comply.

If Richard had said no to taking Donna to the concert, she could have said, "You have every right to say no, but I am very unhappy about your answer, and I am going to go to the concert without you." Another way she could put it is, "Richard, I am sad about your not wanting to take me to the concert, and I am going without you. What do you think about my solution?"

What Donna must not say is: "You are wrong and insensitive for not taking me." That would mean that Donna was equating Richard's cherishing her with obedience to her will, which is wrong! Richard has a right to control his giving. She can accept or reject him but not control him.

If the male energy is smart, he will compromise with the

female for better results, rather than demand unconditional compliance. And, if a woman is a feeling-centered feminine energy, she will hear out her man's input graciously and use as much of his solution as she can. At the same time, he accepts her right to incorporate his suggestions into her own solution. Equations that are all or nothing, black or white, create confrontations that ruin intimacy and romance.

An egomaniacal, dictator type of man (whose woman is unworthy of being cherished because she allows him to act like a tin god without the slightest resistance) is one who believes that his ideas and beliefs are to be rigidly adhered to, without feeling input from his woman and children.

This type of man doesn't want to hear "I like it," "I am afraid," "I am uncomfortable," etc. He doesn't care about her feelings, or, at least, he cares more about his own. He is narcissistic and uncommittable.

An important thing to remember if you choose to be the feminine energy is to never tell a negative feeling to your masculine man, unless you are willing to follow his requested solution or give your solution and ask his thoughts on it. It is frustrating for him to hear a problem and not be able to solve it.

Shan, a legal secretary who believed she was about to get fired, often came home from work in a bad mood. When she would see her boyfriend, Tony, a computer salesman, she'd start telling him how awful things were at work. As soon as she'd begin to talk, he'd interrupt her with suggestions about how to handle the situation. Shan would then get frustrated, saying she only wanted him to listen, and he would get angry and stomp off.

Shan would have done better saying, "Tony, I need to dump some of my feelings about work. I don't really need or want any solutions because I have a plan already. Do you think you can listen for fifteen minutes?"

Tony then knows what is expected, and he can clearly say yes or no to her request. Shan can wail away without fear of his interfering with the venting process.

If she wants his input, she must ask for it by saying, "Tony, I have some negative feelings about this work situation that I want to talk about with you and hopefully get some feedback and suggestions. Are you willing to do this now, or at another time today?" By speaking in this way, Shan is clearly indicating what she wants in a respecting manner that allows Tony to control his destiny and cherish her at the same time.

FEELING WOMEN KNOW WHAT THEY DON'T WANT RATHER THAN WHAT THEY WANT

I believe feminine women should know what they don't want rather than what they want. Knowing what you want is male and logical and often overrides feelings and sensibilities. To know what you don't want requires looking inside yourself, at all of your options, and "feeling" your way toward them. Feminine women "feel" their way into and out of deals, conversations, and situations. If it feels right, do it.

As a feminine woman, you must rely on your feelings to tell you what is good or bad, and then use your brain to act on those feelings. You will get what you want by knowing what feels good or bad, but primarily by knowing what feels *bad* and then saying no to that which does not feel right.

If you rely only on your "thinking, wanting" brain, you can often be persuaded by a man's logical arguments to do things like have casual sex, loan him money, or let him move in, which ultimately won't feel good, and which you will regret. Sometimes a man will challenge you by saying, "Aren't you a nineties woman—smart, assertive, and self-sufficient? Why are you running away without talking about it?" What he is really saying (on another level) is: "Stay in this debate until my logic overrides your feelings." Don't do it!

Not only must you, as a feminine woman, *not* compete logically with masculine men, but it is important that you not explain or defend your feelings. If the man in your life asks you to do something you don't want to do, instead of arguing or defending your position, say, "I appreciate your idea; however, I don't feel good about it. I don't want to do it, and I won't. Will you accept this?"

Most women will feel obliged to explain themselves so they don't sound inflexible, stubborn, hysterical, or stupid.

Leona, a high school art teacher, felt so guilty when asked by her long-term boyfriend, James, an engineer, to do something she was unable to comply with that she would attempt to assuage what she assumed was his disappointment by endlessly explaining why what he asked was impossible. Finally James would snap at her in frustration. Then Leona, believing that his anger was because of her saying no, would continue to defend her position, desperately trying to convince him that her refusal was logical. But, in fact, James was angry at the talk-talk-talk technique that Leona employed, not at her saying no.

Leona and James came to one of my seminars, and I worked with them both onstage. I suggested a new way for James to ask Leona to do something he wanted her to do: "Leona, you may or may not want to do this, and it's okay with me either way. I want to get into the car and head out of town for a weekend—no plans, just spontaneously. What are your feelings about this?"

Then I taught Leona a response that would smoothly handle her saying no to James if she felt that way: "James, your idea is wonderful and sounds like fun. I feel guilty about telling you that this weekend is not good for me because I promised to help a friend move. Do you think you and I can get away the following weekend?"

Both Leona and James needed to accept the other's right to ask for something and to say no, graciously. They both quickly learned this lesson and incorporated this better means of communication into their lives.

Sue Ellen, a beautiful business analyst, always had trouble saying no to men she was attracted to, and the result was that her boyfriend, Bryon, a good-looking stockbroker, easily manipulated her into doing things his way. He would swamp her with humor, affection, and seduction until she gave in to him on any issue, such as having sex when she was ready to walk out the door for work, or staying with him to help him clean his closets instead of going out with her girlfriends on a Saturday-afternoon shopping spree, and most painful of all to her, acquiescing in his delay in talking about their future.

Sue Ellen and Bryon had been "dating" for one and a half years, and Sue Ellen was ready to talk about marriage, but any time she brought up the subject, he would skillfully maneuver her out of it.

"Sue Ellen," he would say, "I love you. You love me. We are having a great relationship. Don't rock the boat. When the time is right, we will get engaged. Trust me."

Although Bryon always spoke with humor and warmth and included lots of hugs, and Sue Ellen always ended up a frustrated but laughing heap in his arms, inside she felt awful. She was angry each time he diverted the conversation, but she didn't know what to do about it.

In time Sue Ellen learned to honor her negative feelings and to communicate them to Bryon. She said, "Bryon, I have loved our relationship for a year and a half. However, I'm feeling very frustrated and intimidated by your unwillingness to talk seriously about what you want for our future. I don't want to devote much more time to this level of commitment. I will stay with you as long as I can, but I'm warning you that I'm running out of good feelings about us. Will you talk with me about this soon?"

Unfortunately, Bryon became angry when Sue Ellen stood her ground and his "techniques" for cajoling her failed. He left in a huff, telling her she was lucky to have him and challenging her to find a better man.

Sue Ellen was shocked to find that instead of intense depression, she was actually relieved that she no longer had to endure the oppression of Bryon's emotional control. The only thing she really missed, she realized, was their fun sex.

I asked Sue Ellen to duty-date until she met a man who was willing and even eager to hear both her negative and positive feelings and to be there with her in a mutually beneficial relationship. I reminded her that if she could learn how to convey to a masculine man what she doesn't want, he would figure out what she *does* want, by investing time, money, and energy. It would be good for him to solve the problem, and he would feel good about himself when he was appreciated as a giving, protective, cherishing man.

Masculine men like problems, challenges, the chase. "Little boys" like Mama to do their work for them. You must decide which you are, a woman who simply and courteously says no to what she does not want, or a powerful woman who cajoles a man into doing it or not doing it her way.

WHY A FEMININE WOMAN SHOULD NEVER ASK A MASCULINE MAN HOW HE FEELS

It is natural that a woman who is feeling-centered would want to use the mode that is most natural and comfortable to her. But if you have chosen to be the feminine energy and are with a man who wants to lead with ideas, suggestions, and opinions, do not ask him about his feelings.

Why? Because all you will get is: "Fine. Okay. Why do you ask?" You will always do better if you tell him your feelings openly and ask him what he thinks and wants to do about them.

Men who want to be respected will often dodge the point when asked how they feel. They may not be "fine" or "okay" at all, but they don't want to open up because it feels too vulnerable. Masculine men need time to think before they talk or act on their feelings, especially when building a relationship with a woman they love.

A masculine man knows that a woman will either provide a safe place for his feelings or hurt them, so generally the man who wants to be respected will hold his cards close to his chest. But he will open up voluntarily once you have created a nonthreatening arena for him. Of course, feminine-energy men who are aware of their feelings and want to be cherished *always* want to talk about them and have you (the masculine-energy female) listen and help.

There is nothing wrong with either man, but you must remember your priorities in the relationship to avoid problems later. If you want to be respected first as the masculine energy, and he does, too, conflict could lead to collision, competition, and confusion. Similarly, if being cherished is your first priority and his first priority also, same problem. It won't work.

When a man or woman wants respect as the first priority, he or she often feels manipulated when asked questions about his or her feelings, especially questions that elicit fear, guilt, inadequacy, and other sensitive issues. When people want to be cherished, they will ask for cherishing. But when a man talks about his problems to you, you run the risk of becoming "Mom," "sob sister," or "therapist," all of which eliminate you as his woman. "Little boy" men can have sex with a "big mama," but men who want respect for their problem-solving skills will turn off.

When a man feels safe, he will share his feelings voluntarily. Until then, don't ask. The male energy who is respected will feel cherished. The female energy who is cherished will feel respected. Cherishing at its best is freely given, not asked for. All too often, however, women make the mistake of complaining to men who don't give, protect, or cherish enough.

Do not ask to be cherished. If you don't feel cherished, leave quietly. If he wants you, he will come and get you and give you what you want, often by observing you and fulfilling your desires even before you think of them.

Tricia, a gorgeous aerobics instructor who attended one of my seminars, was confused and upset when she asked, "Why does my boyfriend, Phil, get mad at me when I ask him to make love? Isn't it flattering to him to feel wanted by me?"

I knew that Phil, who was a trainer at the same gym at which Tricia worked, was responding from his maleness. Phil wanted to give lovemaking to Tricia. He did not want to perform on demand. It felt insulting to him, a power play for control.

I always tell women who want to be the feminine energy to magnetize lovemaking by being sensuously affectionate, sexually attractive. To signal a man sensuously but nonerotically that you are available and receptive will get the message across if he is a man who wants to give you pleasure of all types, particularly making love. For both Tricia and Phil to have equal rights to ask for sex caused a collision of wills. Phil wanted to be respected as the initiator, and eventually Tricia liked being the responder to him.

By allowing Phil the safety to decide when and where he wanted to initiate sex, Tricia avoided "turning him off" by jumping the gun and not waiting. This passivity might seem like negative manipulation, but I believe it is as positive a manipulation as wearing makeup, dressing seductively, or acting like a lady. "Going for it" without consideration for a man's need to be respected is the fastest way to turn him off.

Do you want to leave your power plays at the office or take them home and play hardball with your mate? I suggest that one of you leave your power at the office, while the other bring it home potently.

A patient woman can magnetize all the love, affection, time, and lovemaking out of a man without verbally asking for it. In romance, complements attract; people who are similar repel each other. What's your choice?

WOMEN WHO TALK TOO MUCH

If you have chosen to be the feminine, receptive energy in your relationship, then *shut up* even when you ache to fill in the empty spaces in a conversation. Your masculine man will set the tone and fill the spaces according to his wants and needs. You need only respond, relax, relinquish control, and follow. He will get overwhelmed if you fill every moment with sound. Too much data coming into your right-handed man's brain will cause him to shut down.

If you cannot let him lead you in conversation, perhaps you really want to be the masculine energy, and if so, keep talking and let him listen and be your feminine counterpart.

HOW TO TURN HIM INTO A WIMP

The most damaging thing you can do to your respected man is to assume that you can solve his problems, i.e., with his job, health, taxes, banking, family, ex-wife and kids. You have every right to be "the man"—generous, protective, and cherishing—as long as you and he consciously recognize the roles you are taking.

Secure, feminine women take care of their side of the relationship by sharing feelings and vetoing immoral and unethical requests. *Passive patience is the feminine way.* Assertive action is the masculine way. Don't jump back and forth. Stay in one place until asked to do otherwise, and then only do what feels good for you to do.

ON WANTING "DADDY"

Often, a woman in pain will say, "George, I am in pain over ———. What are *you* going to do to fix it?"

She is asking her man to be Daddy, not boyfriend or husband. Protective men automatically will give a solution to their women in pain and expect them to at least consider it. A woman who resents his giving solutions only wants to live in the problem or have him do what it takes to make her happy without her participation. A masculine husband or boyfriend expects his woman to ask for advice or to solve her problems on her own; he does not expect her to ask him to solve a problem as if she were a helpless child.

Amy, an aspiring actress who enjoys being the feminine energy, really cared about her boyfriend, Dennis, a successful audio engineer, but she resented him, too, because he would not solve her problems. She would ask him to call her agent for her and chew him out over auditions she felt she was not being set up for. Although he was willing to listen to her problem, Dennis told Amy that she should call her agent herself. He said he would give her advice and opinions about her business decisions only after she put her solutions on the table in an adult manner. He would not be her "daddy," and of course, because he required her to be an adult, businesslike woman, she gained a lot of inner, anchored security.

Amy learned that she didn't need Dennis's assistance to be respectable and decisive in her career. Everyone is masculine at work, i.e., they must negotiate and objectively deal with situations and ask for help only when it is appropriate. To be feminine does not mean to be helpless.

If a man gives you advice that you know will not work, you cannot blindly follow him. Instead, use one of the Communication tools that is used for conflict, in this case, Stroke and Stand.

Say, "[Name], I like it when you give me the advice I ask for; however, I feel uncomfortable about doing [whatever he suggested], because [give your reasons]. Are you willing to talk more about your ideas, thoughts, and suggestions until I am comfortable making my decision?"

To receive as much data from your man as he can give allows you to make a better decision. When a feminine woman like Amy is with a man whose brains she respects, it is appropriate to glean his opinions, ideas, and suggestions. But it is not appropriate to use his ideas as directives to be followed. "Macho" men are dictators who order and demand adherence to their wishes because they feel insecure and inadequate with a secure and adequate woman. A masculine, healthy, sensitive man enjoys assisting his woman in her own career but accepts her final decision as her right, not as disrespectful rebellion. Arguing and debating painfully are not the goals—talking, sharing, and mutual respecting are.

In their personal, intimate life, Dennis did take charge and expected Amy to follow his lead, but not in the area of her career. He respected this area of her life and supported her masculine decisive energy, even when she didn't. Too much feminine energy is as bad as too much masculine energy. Balance is appropriate.

Dennis had integrity as a man, and he did not allow Amy to seduce him into being "Daddy," even when she was upset with his refusal. A man and woman of virtue can *negotiate* their love affair as good human beings. They walk through their natural, normal fears of rejection and abandonment to the final conclusion, whether it is a failure of compatibility or successful intimacy.

DON'T HOLD BACK

Men and women who are comfortable in themselves practice integrity and virtue. They openly share and discuss what they want and what they don't want and learn from their mistakes.

A man who is virtuous and has integrity takes the time to think through his priorities and goals and articulates them, so that a woman can know him and hear him clearly. If he is without virtue or integrity, he allows his fears of rejection to intimidate him into lying or manipulating.

Men who take pride in their clear-thinking "left-lobe" logic can be turned off by a manipulative woman who is dishonest about her true feelings. A man can understand and handle a woman who is having a screaming fit better than he can a cool, calm woman who is telling white lies or giving false information about her feelings. Women who are virtuous and have integrity *tell how they feel*, moment to moment, even if this varies constantly. A man can track feelings that are honest, and he can trust that woman, because he gets a moment-to-moment weather report. So, remember, don't hold in your negative feelings. Say no, and don't explain or defend your feelings.

The Imperfect Phase
(3–6 Months)

CHAPTER 12

Dealing with the Toad in Every Prince

The Imperfect Phase begins about sixty days into the relationship. At this point, people usually feel comfortable enough with each other to get off their best behavior and, in effect, "be themselves." This is when you learn what you already knew but didn't want to admit, that nobody is perfect, including your newfound love. It is kind of like autumn in that things start to cool down a bit.

The purpose of this relationship phase is to find out what your negotiable and nonnegotiable items are, what you do and do not like about the other person, while you are revealing yourself. You both need to know the whole person, the good and the bad, before you can negotiate a future together. Otherwise, you are negotiating with only half a person.

People who have a fear of intimacy, the "Ninety-Day Wonders," usually abort the relationship during this period. I call it "abort," because as soon as the Perfect Phase is over, they run off to again look for that perfect person. These Ninety-Day Wonders are just as often women as men, and one reason why so many women are unattached or are not in fulfilling relationships is that they overidealize a man.

The Imperfect Phase creeps up on people gradually. It usually starts with little things. Maybe you're out driving one day, and he is at the wheel. Suddenly someone cuts in front of him on the road, and he starts shouting and driving like a madman. No longer is he the gentle giant he appeared to be in those red-hot and rosy early days of the relationship. He's become a red-eyed monster, taking you with him on his kamikaze ride. You are now seeing a side of him that he has been hiding for months.

Or maybe he takes you to a nice restaurant, and all of a sudden he criticizes an inept waiter to the point that you want to slide under the table. Or maybe you visit his apartment, which he has been bragging about, and you find it tacky and tasteless.

It is at this point that the perfect projection starts to fade. Sadness creeps in. He isn't perfect. In fact, he's very imperfect. So where does that leave you—and what are you to do? Accept? Reject? Tolerate? Rebuild?

There are three ways you can relate to your man.

1. You can *accept* him, which means that you may not always like or approve of what he is and does, but you find more assets than liabilities and you want to stay with him. To accept is to love someone even when you don't always approve of his behavior.
2. You can *reject* him, which means that there are irreconcilable differences between you that you cannot, in good conscience, get past. To reject is to love someone enough to let him go to someone else who does accept him as he is.
3. You can *tolerate* him, which is to half-accept (love) and half-reject (dislike) him. This is a process of teeter-tottering back and forth. It promotes mood swings that are difficult for you both. To tolerate is the only destructive thing in a romance. When you tolerate lateness, sloppiness, burps, expelling of gas, lying, selfishness, cheating, cheapness, or insensitivity, etc., you hurt yourself, by failing your own virtue and sense of integrity.

Narcissists of either sex tolerate others' imperfections from their place of perfection. To be around these people is to live under a microscope. They constantly attempt to teach, preach, criticize, and rebuild others to their standards, and of course they fail and move on. When they meet their match, another perfect narcissist, the war is on.

Do not try to rebuild your man. When you scrutinize his clothes, his apartment, his hairstyle, his grammar—all those things that make up his essence—and then try to rebuild him, you are acting like a mother, and you are using masculine energy. If you get the job done, he becomes your feminine man, and you may lose respect for him, while he gains respect for you at the cost of cherishing you. Whatever you find missing in him, you can get from other sources.

If he isn't crazy about ballet, go with a girlfriend or relative. If he doesn't have a jacket you like, give him one for his birthday or Christmas. If his apartment is a designer's nightmare, entertain in yours and wait until you are engaged or married and living together before you redesign his place. In other words, let him be who he is until you and he are a team, and then negotiate for changes. Remember, he may have some things he'd like you to do differently, as well.

So you have only two choices: to accept him as he is, as long as he has one or two of the nonnegotiable items you require, and he is moral and ethical, or reject him cleanly and kindly. Do not try to retrain him through criticism, which damages his image of you as a sensitive, receptive, accepting woman and does little good. If a man's assets outweigh his liabilities, go for it. If not, get out early.

There is someone for everyone, except the narcissist. Narcissists would rather be alone anyway with their perfect selves instead of compromising. Of course, many women simply don't have the maturity or staying power to look beyond a man's imperfections or the sense to realize that it is a man's imperfections that individualize him, give him character, and, finally, make him lovable.

To have a real relationship that lasts, you must start with an image of what you want in a man. I call these the "nonnegotiable" items. You must decide how important to you are such things as intelligence, good looks, a great body, money, education, family ties, humor, religion, ethics, or culture. The same goes for great sex or health, housekeeping abilities, handyman abilities, or politics. The list goes on to include anything else you want in your man.

The problem you face is how many nonnegotiable items are appropriate. Usually I advise one or two and that you get flexible about whatever else is negotiable. If you need a perfect partner, you are a narcissist, and unconsciously you really want to be single and independent.

Anabelle, a waitress in a coffeehouse, absolutely needed intelligence in a man (nonnegotiable item) and got it in Frank, a college professor who taught Greek philosophy. He wasn't the best dresser she had ever met, or the best dancer, but he did have brains, and she melted every time he talked Greek philosophy.

Frank had been looking for an earthy woman who would enjoy creating a home for herself and him. Anabelle was not his intellectual equal, but she had his nonnegotiable item—sensuousness and great sexuality. The rest he could get over lunch on campus.

Hilary, who worked in an art gallery, had three nonnegotiable items: good looks, gregariousness, and sensuality. Harvey, a painter, had all three. It did not matter to either of them that she had more money than he did.

Harvey's nonnegotiable item was social flair. He needed people around him who were cultured, interesting, and as good conversationalists as he was. Hilary had all three qualities, and she had wonderful friends whom he enjoyed. Although Hilary was five years older than Harvey, her age was of no concern to him, nor was her angular and somewhat plain face. They were committed and in love and fit together. That was all that mattered to them, even if some others could not see them as an appropriate match.

Basically, we are attracted to someone in three ways: physically (sensually and sexually), mentally (a person's financial success, education, intelligence, communication skills), and emotionally (a person's warmth, lovability). We would like all three in good equal measure, but the best anyone can hope for is satisfaction with two out of three. Some people will take one quality out of three as long as it compensates for the other two.

If he's handsome and smart, he's probably broke. Or he may be rich and smart, but ugly. He may be ugly and weird, but also rich. He may be dumb and cold, but he turns you on. If that's okay with you, it's okay with me.

Remember, we all have our weird aspects. We are all broken in one way or another, and we must learn to accept the broken aspect in order to love. It's easy to love the perfect one that does not exist. Accept what you can in your mate—otherwise no one would ever stay in a relationship. The secret is to find out what the other person's downsides are, and whether you can live with them. Consider carefully and be wise and use those God-given smarts of yours.

Every day I listen to someone who traded in a person they would now die for. If he wears polyester, you can buy him silk after you get him. If he's overweight but not grossly so, make love with him so often that he gets thin from happiness. I feel that if you get someone who is 51 percent or better, *keep him*. That is to say, if you like more about the person than you don't, then go for it. Because odds are that if you don't, and you go out looking for a better deal elsewhere, you could end up with someone who is only 49 percent or worse.

There is a prince in every toad and a toad in every prince. But does someone fall in love with the prince part of a person? No way. They fall in love with the toad part. It is the idiosyncrasies and weirdness that really endears someone to you, the part that makes you say, "Oh, that's just him," and you love him anyway.

I tell women that if they are still waiting for the perfect man—mentally, physically, emotionally—he's not coming. That's the message I had to teach Sheila, and she has thanked me for it.

Sheila, a pretty trust officer in a bank, had fantasized about being married to a tall, dark, rich man who wanted her desperately and would do anything to have her. She had dated a number of men through the years, almost becoming engaged once some years back, but never to her dream man. Now, at thirty-five, she was getting a little anxious about ever marrying or having children, and so she put out the word to friends and relatives to begin beating the bushes for "the right man."

Her friends came up with Stan, an accountant who, although slightly bald on top, was decent, successful, and charming.

But when Sheila met Stan on the blind date their mutual friends had arranged, she did not want him. Bald turns me off, she thought. I like a man with a full head of hair.

Stan didn't want Sheila, either, when he saw her, because she was about ten pounds overweight. Fat I don't need, he thought. I want gorgeous.

At thirty-eight, Stan was ready to settle down and marry after years of bachelorhood. His taste in women had been fast and loose—good girls need not apply—and he'd loved every moment of it. But now he saw that all his friends were married, starting families, and living that quiet good life of fatherhood, family, and fraternity that made him feel isolated and shut out of the mainstream. So now he wanted a good, smart, virtuous woman, but still one who was gorgeous.

The date looked as though it was going to be a disaster. Sheila and Stan both prayed for an early end to the evening. But because of the effects of a heavy rain and mud slide, they were stuck together inside a cozy restaurant for hours. When they both realized how long they would be together, they relaxed and began to have fun.

And guess what? They really liked one another. Still, they didn't look at all like what the other one wanted, and at the end of the evening they were confused about what to do. He wanted Julia Roberts, and she wanted Richard Gere.

Would they set aside their idealized versions of the perfect mate in the face of reality, or would they chase their ghostly lovers into middle-aged loneliness and eventually settle for even less than the perceived value of each other?

What happened was that Sheila and Stan chose to continue to see each other. As their dating progressed, they liked more and more of what they saw. Still, their hang-ups and fantasies prevailed; and so they sought counseling from me, and we discussed their negotiable and nonnegotiable requirements for a mate. They began to realize what a good thing they had, what was really important to them, and how *love* is internal not external, how it is spiritual not material, and that they were falling in love with real people, not fabricated characters on a movie screen.

After one year, Sheila and Stan married and are a very happy couple. We've spent some great evenings together laughing about their early "projections" of each other, and we have become a little tearful about how close they came to losing each other.

Here's a pledge I often ask both women and men to take:

"I PROMISE TO ACCEPT MYSELF AND ALL OTHER HUMAN BEINGS AS IMPERFECT AND ACCEPTABLE THAT WAY."

MAINTAIN YOUR PRIMARY ROLE

I find that one of the biggest problems during the Imperfect Phase is maintaining your primary roles.

In the Perfect Phase, you have each played your appropriate traditional roles; he chased you, so he was the "male," and you responded, so you were the "female." Or you played your nontraditional roles (you chased him, so you are the male and he the female). But when the Imperfect Phase rolls in, both of you find that your natural tendencies, drives, and behaviors start reasserting themselves. You will have to deal with the issue of equality—both wanting equal respect for your thinking and both wanting your feelings cherished.

It is difficult to restrict normal, natural behavior. If you have evolved to the point where you are highly respected and also very sensitive, it feels unnatural and contrived to promote the "rational" side over the "emotional," or vice versa. But when you neglect doing this one-legged dance, you will step on his toes, and the dance will soon end.

Sheri was such a woman. She was a bright, sensitive lawyer who wanted to marry. Sheri heard about my system and began using it on dates. She wanted to be the feminine energy, but keeping her bright, witty mouth under control was maddeningly difficult with Claude, an investment banker. She *really* wanted Claude and felt the compulsion to tell him all about herself, afraid that if he didn't know how great she was, he would be bored and leave.

So Sheri ceased to act "feminine" and began talking to Claude about her many accomplishments. This totally earned her his respect, as well as a business opportunity—they did a deal together. But she lost him as a possible boyfriend. Later, she admitted her mistake and went back "on the program" and eventually met and married her man.

Some women are Miss Docile for about three months and then they feel secure enough to try to take over the raft, to try to force their man to be passive and feminine. Masculine men sometimes let their women get away with this for a few months during this Imperfect Phase, hoping that Miss Docile will return. But when the next period—the Negotiable Phase—begins, the man and woman begin to fight for control over their lives, which either ends the relationship or results in one or the other capitulating resentfully, generally out of addiction to the sex in the relationship. Either way, intimacy is ruined even if they marry.

HIDING THE DARK SIDE

Another problem common to all relationships is that we hide our defects and dark side behind a wall of superficial perfection until time and circumstance force them out.

Sally, a manicurist, was messy. She wouldn't clean her house or do laundry, or even bother to get dressed if she didn't have to.

Of course Len, her new man of seventy-two days who owned a body shop, was a neatnik, as karmic law always seems to set up.

Sally, who was crazy about Len, wasn't taking any chances, and so she successfully hid her slothful ways, managing to make him believe that she was as neat and perfect as he was.

During the first few weeks of their relationship, she managed to dress up when he came to call for her, and she stuffed excess items in closets and under the bed. She convinced him that she preferred going to his apartment across town because it was on the way from her office. This worked out well, because Len liked entertaining her at his place and felt very comfortable being in charge.

A problem arose one Saturday afternoon, when Len was driving around Sally's neighborhood and decided to drop in on her unannounced. He rang her bell.

The rueful and embarrassed woman who opened her front door only at his insistence could not be his Sally. *His* Sally didn't run around with dirty hair, in a sweat suit, as messy and unkempt as her house appeared to be. Len's shocked reaction caused her to burst into tears. She was sure he would reject her on the spot.

Luckily, Len proved to have a sense of humor, and he took her into his arms, where Sally sank gratefully.

Sally's mistake was in always trying to please rather than being herself. She was dependent upon Len's approval until she and Len let their romantic expectations of the other fade in favor of a real relationship of good and bad, up and down, perfect and imperfect. Of course Len would probably never have looked once at Sally if she had been sloppy and dirty when they met, so Sally decided to mend at least some of her ways in order to keep Len happy and sexually attracted to her.

NO PERFECT PEOPLE

I advise women and men to say, "I am imperfect and he/she is also." We are all defective, so commit to the relationship and do your best on your side of the equation. This way, on the bad days you don't look at the person but rather to the survival of the *relationship*. You must think, I must carry my part, even when the person I am with doesn't.

We all have qualities we could eliminate or improve, but we rarely will when a gun is put to our head. Humans grow and bloom in loving, accepting relationships. When you see your lover doing "that thing" that you hate, ask yourself whether "that thing" is bad enough to reject him for, and then either accept him or reject him.

In the meantime, share your feelings gently by saying, "You have every right to do *that thing*, but I am uncomfortable with it. Will you consider changing or disciplining yourself?"

When people are loved and accepted, they can "hear" what you are saying and they can choose either to modify their behavior or to pay the price of rejection by you. When you criticize or hassle people, you are being righteous and judgmental and exhibiting *your* dark side.

Does rejection mean the end of the relationship? Not necessarily. When you come across a behavior that you know you cannot approve of, you can talk about it, using the tools of communication in this book.

Susan, a secretary, could not accept the indiscriminate cursing of her boyfriend, Harry, but she tolerated it because he had many qualities that kept her interested. Then she heard me talk about how destructive it was to their relationship for her to tolerate him. She chose to reject his behavior without ending the relationship.

She said, "Harry, you have every right to constantly curse, but I am uncomfortable when you do it. I am going to walk away until you stop. Okay?"

It was okay with Harry. An auto mechanic, he'd picked up the habit at work, didn't really like it, and in his heart, wanted her to signal him. He soon stopped cursing and they continued their very good relationship.

Joanna, an assistant marketing manager, disliked the fact that her boyfriend, Donald, an architect, would plan things for them to do without consulting her. She said, "Don, you really do plan fun times for us, but I am uncomfortable when you don't find out how I feel about your plans. If you don't check with me, I will automatically say, 'No, thank you.' "

Don got angry for a while, but he, too, learned to modify his behavior.

Don't lecture, argue, put down, or criticize. Take a position and anchor yourself. This idea of accepting or rejecting rather than tolerating him and his imperfections is a big part of getting married. When you are committed and want to be married, you are like two people on a life raft in a turbulent sea. Each of you has one paddle, not two, and you are each rowing on one side of the raft, not both. You are dependent on each other for power and direction. Any excess power plays will cause the raft to go in circles. Balanced energy is the name of the marriage game.

One of the reasons I suggest that you do not live with a man until you are engaged or married is so that during times of stress you can pull away for a while until things cool off. Go to your own apartment, take a walk, hang up the phone, talk later, look the other way. Save total rejection for moral and ethical issues such as dishonesty or violence, or if he is a chronic cad or displays insensitive behavior. Total rejection is for things that, if you stay, indicate your complicity.

Little faults deserve little rejections and lots of love both ways.

CHAPTER 13

How to Handle Conflict

N ow I want to teach you how to handle *conflict*, which is any difference of ideas or feelings about an action to be taken that results in a dispute. In other words, anytime you both want to be respected for your ideas, or cherished for feelings, you are in conflict. You need to use careful, objective negotiation and communication tools. Here are some tools for conflict resolution.

STROKE AND STAND
(FOR IMMEDIATE RESPONSE TO A PAINFUL SITUATION)

Although Beth, a model, was beautiful and articulate, she had difficulty getting in touch with her painful feelings. She had even more difficulty sharing them with her boyfriend, Fred, a management consultant.

Because of her inability to say no to Fred, he thought she always agreed with whatever he said or did. When he believed a conflict was imminent, he became logical, slipping into his courtroom ways, while she became illogical and overemotional. She did try to share her painful feelings with Fred, but she botched the process to the point where Fred could not "hear" her because she was so emotional. As he tried to question her to find out what she intended to say, his irritated frustration intimidated her back into silence.

Beth needed a clear way to speak to Fred about how she felt while she was under the pressure of his strength.

She joined a weekly class I was teaching for women, with the idea of finding out how to speak up for herself.

In the women's group, I suggested we make believe that Fred wanted to take Beth to a concert of a group she really didn't care for.

I talked about the first tool for conflict resolution: Stroke and Stand—that is, always make a man feel accepted. Tell him he has the right (freedom) to do or say anything as long as it is moral (not hurting your body) or ethical (not hurting your money, property, or career). This grounds a woman and keeps her from "reacting" in a rebellious way. Example:

1. Stroke—"Fred, you have the right to decide that we will go to that concert."
2. Stand—Now she has to tell him her feelings clearly so that he will hear and cherish her feelings, unless he is a self-centered narcissist who doesn't care about sharing, in which case it is better to find out now, not later, after marriage.

    "However, I don't like that group's music. I find it off-putting.

    The stand shows your self-love: You have told him what you don't want.
3. Contract—Now Beth can offer him a possible alternative, in a respectful way.

    "Fred, what do you think about going this weekend with Zac who really likes their music? I will feel really special if you take me to see a movie tonight, one that we would both enjoy. What do you say?"

Whether Fred does or doesn't take Beth to the concert is immaterial. They can work out their schedules. What does matter is that he respond to her with love and sensitivity.

"Beth, of course I care about your feelings about this concert. Your feelings are a priority for me. I'm willing to work out a deal so both of us are happy."

Being in a relationship with a selfish narcissist, someone who doesn't care about your feelings, is "doormat" training and is not acceptable to any woman in today's enlightened society. This kind of relationship only works when one person *needs* the other at any cost, and you don't want that. The game played by narcissistic men is to have their ideas approved of by their partner whether or not that partner really agrees. You'd best exit this situation.

Beth did not want to limit Fred's freedom, nor did she want to control him, or have him control her. But she did want to control *herself* physically, mentally, and emotionally while in his space. That is her right, and a sign of good mental health.

The Stroke and Stand technique allowed Beth to speak up when such incidents happened and smoothed the way for her and Fred to become more deeply attached, and ultimately engaged.

Here is another way to use this technique:

Imagine that Fred had the habit not only of looking at pretty women when he was out with Beth, but also of pointing them out to her, which made her feel negative and undesirable.

She could say [Stroke]: "Fred, you have every right to look at pretty women and point them out to me, but [Stand] I feel *jealous* when you do that, and I don't want to feel that way. So if you continue [Contract], I will be leaving."

Of course, then if he continues, she must leave, because it clearly means that he does not cherish her feelings. A woman of integrity stands by her contract.

FIVE-STEP CLEANUP (FOR DELAYED RESPONSE TO A PAINFUL SITUATION)

Marsha, a quiet, pretty, successful insurance broker in the Midwest, was going with Peter, the manager of an automotive-parts concern.

Because they were planning a vacation in Hawaii, and Peter was very busy at work while Marsha wasn't, he asked her to research and select an island for them to use as "home base" for their other island-hopping trips. Although Marsha readily agreed, after a few weeks she told Peter she was unable to choose one because they all seemed so nice. She asked *him* to pick one instead.

Peter selected an island, which Marsha accepted, but then, at the moment they reached their hotel room, she wistfully commented in her gentle way, "Gee, I wish we had picked another island. There's nothing to do here." No criticizing or confronting him, just this slight disappointment, which, of course, brought Peter down for quite a while.

Marsha was passive-aggressive. Asserting herself to get something she enjoyed, or saying no, was nerve-racking for her. Instead, she would say yes to almost anything and then sabotage things later by being unhappy and showing it. By doing this, she remained in "control" of the situation, in an undercover way. Marsha needed to learn how to bring up negative, fearful subjects and feelings.

When Marsha attended a seminar I gave in the city where she lived, I taught her the "Five-Step Cleanup," using a situation she always feared—telling Peter she wanted to go on a weekend trip with a couple of her friends, which meant she wouldn't be seeing him, a problem, since Marsha had trouble "abandoning" Peter for a whole weekend.

1. Ask for Permission to Enter His Space.
    "Peter, I want to talk to you about my going away next weekend with Gail and Vickie. Do you want to talk now or later?"
    Feeling respected, Peter hopefully will set a time now or later to talk. He will feel comfortable and not bombarded by Marsha, who has not triggered a "left-lobe" argument between her male energy and his male brain. This will help her case.
2. Give a Stroke of Recognition for His Good Aspects.
    "Peter, I really appreciate how much you want me to have fun and feel good."

3. Share Your Feelings.

By doing this, Marsha gives Peter a chance to love her and cherish her. She is allowing herself to be vulnerable.

"However, I'm feeling guilty about going away and leaving you alone this weekend, though it's something I will enjoy."

4. Share Your *Not Wants* First, to Get Your *Wants*.

"Peter, I don't want to see you as a warden and resent you, so I am going away in spite of my feelings."

5. Use the Contract.

"Peter, are you okay about my leaving?"

All answers are either *yes* or *no.* Any questions, debates, accusations, criticisms, are blocks. In this case Peter does care about Marsha and cherishes her feelings, so he will either

1. Say a clean yes, or
2. Explain his reasons for saying no and hopefully work with Marsha to create a compromise.

If Peter were the type of man who avoided a clean negotiation in order to intimidate her out of her weekend, Marsha could respond with a Stroke-and-Stand tool.

"Peter, you have every right to avoid a straight yes or no. I don't want to fight. I will take care of myself. I will put up with this kind behavior as long as I can, but then I will leave."

By saying the above, Marsha would have given Peter the "price" for his use of intimidation or seduction. It is up to him to negotiate a clean compromise or say yes or no. Otherwise, *he will pay the price of ultimately losing Marsha.*

A woman must not allow herself to be swept up in the game of "uproar," and run around in circles of explanations and accusations that blot out feelings. A woman like Marsha who has extreme sensitivity to others' feelings must use her "left lobe" and think through her feelings of guilt and fear so that she can avoid sabotaging intimacy again. "Not rocking the boat" and delaying conflict always lead to a bigger conflict later. Sharing her feelings moment by moment helped Peter love and cherish her better.

A masculine-energy woman who wants to use this Five-Step Cleanup tool should lead with her thoughts and wants in order to avoid painful fights over who is leading and who is responding. When a masculine-energy woman is an indecisive leader who mixes her thoughts and her feeling statements, she confuses her feminine man or she collides with his thoughts and feelings, endangering their future. Remember, the masculine person leads with "I want, I think, how do you feel about it?" and the other tells the truth about his or her feelings and says yes or no openly in order for good communication to take place.

Peter was a good man, and Marsha *became* a good woman using these tools in the relationship.

VALIDATION
(FOR BRINGING UNSPOKEN BODY LANGUAGE TO A VERBAL LEVEL)

This communication tool makes clear the meaning underlying nonverbal body language that we pick up intuitively—his tone of voice, facial expression, posture, and gestures.

Carolyn, a script supervisor for a Hollywood production company, had no problem saying no or asking for what she wanted from Bill, a "strong, silent type" sound mixer, with Latin-lover good looks.

Bill was so attractive that he did not have to chase after women; they chased him. And Carolyn did not chase after men; they chased her. After six months of dancing around each other, waiting for someone to make a move, Bill did, and a loving relationship began.

However, after they had been together for several months, a miserable Carolyn came to see me, explaining that their relationship had begun to come apart because Bill would not talk about what he wanted or what he thought, which the male-energy person must do in order to have good communication with the female-energy person.

Because of this, Carolyn found herself harassing Bill as her way of finding out what he wanted, and Bill had begun to pull back.

When Carolyn wanted to talk about their future together, she would say, "Bill, do you want to be married someday? When?"

But Bill would avoid the subject by answering, "I don't know today. Can you give me more time?"

Bill was interested in marrying Carolyn, but her controlling ways triggered warning signs that he knew well from past relationships. He wanted to see how far she would go to pressure him into talking about marriage. He wanted her to let him pick the time to romantically propose. He did not want to tell her prematurely that he wanted to marry her. He was afraid that would give her ammunition to push him faster.

I taught her to use *Validation*. Carolyn needed to "flush" Bill to a verbal level.

She needed to say, "Bill, I sense that you don't want to talk about our future because you have not answered yes or no to my question. Am I right?"

Now Bill may say yes or no, or he may say nothing. All answers other than yes, are no. They are clean, acceptable, and easily understood. Saying nothing is teasing and baffling and painful, and if Bill doesn't answer, Carolyn should *assume* Bill is saying no. She must then decide her appropriate action—accept or reject him.

I taught Carolyn that whenever she wanted a response from Bill, she should state his position for him respectfully: "I sense [believe] you feel angry, resentful, uncomfortable, etc. Am I right?" By using that approach, she could avoid appearing to control him by demanding answers or actions.

By her saying, "Bill, do you want [*whatever*], or do you not want [*whatever*]," and waiting for him to think about it and then answer, Bill would be in control of himself, and thus more comfortable with her, and this is what he needed to even consider marriage to Carolyn.

The Negotiation
(6–9 Months)

CHAPTER 14

Striking a Deal

In the Perfect Phase, you met the one perfect man on earth for you, and he finally found the woman of his fantasies. Then, in the Imperfect Phase, you found out the truth about his weird habits, and he learned about your nutty obsessions. If, at that point, you still liked each other, but he was not willing to assume responsibilities, or you were not able to give up your independence, one or the other of you probably found ways to end the relationship.

But if you both chose to accept the other, based on the good, the bad, and the in-between, and he (as the male) assumed the responsibility of the relationship, and you (as the female) gave up your independent ways (or vice versa), you will now enter the Negotiation Period of the relationship. It is in the next three months that you will have the opportunity to begin building a long-term relationship commitment (married or not).

The relationship commitment takes over where the commitment to a person ends because a human being cannot be good enough every day to be worthy of a commitment from you. But the relationship can be, and it will keep two committed people together.

LIFE-COMMITMENT QUESTIONS

Although in this period you and he will continue to talk about the same things you have been discussing since the beginning of the relationship, now, in the Negotiation Period, there is a greater weight to resolving things because these are issues that you will live with daily for the rest of your lives. Of course, life means change, and you and he must constantly renegotiate. But negotiating things before trouble strikes eliminates a lot of stress on a couple.

For instance, if you do choose to marry, will it be in a religious or civil ceremony or both? What impact (for life) will this have on your families? What about children? Yes? No? How many? What religion will they be raised in? Or none? What if he already has children and an ex-wife?

If you both have careers that demand a lot of time, and you both want a family, one of you has to decide to put the family first or the career first. Which of you will it be?

If he wants to live in a rural area and you want to live in a big city, you will have to work out either living in a rural area near a big city, or, if you can afford it, living in the city with a weekend country house.

Do you put career as the first priority in where you will live, or will you choose your location based on the family you want to raise? Most masculine-energy men want to make sure that their career is grounded, so most masculine-energy men will want to live near their business. Most feminine-energy women will want the opportunity of having children, while their masculine-energy man carries the major burden of support.

Will you live near your parents, his parents, his children? What financial goals are important? Do you want to live for today and spend, or save for tomorrow?

To reach an understanding and a commitment, each person has to ask four questions:

What do I want?

What do you want?

What do I not want?

What do you not want?

Then you both have to agree.

Frances had a career as an editor in a fast-growing publishing house. She became involved with Luke, who likewise had a prospering career, his in the stock exchange. They had been in their committed relationship for eight months and had begun to negotiate for their future together with plans to marry the next year.

One of the issues they dealt with was whether they would wait for children or have them as soon as possible and get a great au pair so that Frances's career would continue uninterrupted.

They decided to marry, have two children fast, and have someone live in and be with the babies for the next few years while both of them achieved their career goals. Then they would renegotiate if necessary or desirable.

For nine months, Lilith and Martin had been in a relationship in which they were having difficulty negotiating. Although they both knew they wanted to marry someday and start a family, they clashed on the issue of when to marry and whether she would quit her job after the first baby came.

Lilith wanted to marry soon and did not want to continue to work as a paralegal after having a child, but they would need her income, baby or not, to help him through an advanced law degree.

The more Lilith lived with the question, the firmer was her decision that she did not want to let someone else raise her baby.

Their nonnegotiable issues collided, baby now versus money needed now. As a result, the relationship fell apart. Lilith went back to her still-waiting old boyfriend, Jeremy, a travel agent, who was not as well educated as Martin but was ready and willing to marry and start a family now.

For Stewart, an exporter, having a wife who was available at a moment's notice to travel with him to foreign countries was a life-commitment issue. Sylvia, his girlfriend, and he had done just that in the past year and a half of their monogamous relationship, especially after she was laid off from her job in the bridal department of a department store.

In the last few months, their "future talk" (negotiations) had begun in earnest. But the problem was, as much as Sylvia enjoyed their trips, she did not want to be there only for Stewart; she wanted her own career as well.

Both wanted to either move forward or end the relationship. As a solution, Sylvia looked for a storefront in which to begin a bridal shop. She had worked for five years to get enough money to follow her dream. Now she was faced with a decision about a possible marriage to Stewart and his need for her to be available for him.

Their resolution came with Sylvia getting a partner who could be available daily and was willing to have Sylvia come and go as needed. Sylvia and Stewart had successfully negotiated their differences and made these work for the benefit of both of them.

CHANGING ROLES

Flexibility in role behavior is the mode of this period. Each person is "coming out" more individually than in the earlier phases of the relationship, so this is the time when you begin to negotiate an interchanging of masculine and feminine roles.

Sarah, a casting director at a major studio, had always enjoyed driving, and it was difficult for her to maintain her position of passenger in her boyfriend Jed's car during the first seven months of their relationship, but she had done it.

Following my teachings, whenever Jed, an assistant director, would speed or lane-change a little recklessly, she would communicate her feelings of nervousness. He would immediately slow down and take more care. Still, Sarah wanted to do the driving, and she wanted to ask to do it by using my system.

After he agreed to talk about the subject, she said, "Jed, I appreciate your willingness to hear my feelings of nervousness when you drive, and I appreciate your willingness to accommodate my needs. However, I want to do all the driving. What do you think?"

Jed agreed because he knew that when she was comfortable, he would be. It was not necessary for his male ego to maintain control. He could become the (feminine) passenger.

Leo, a graphic designer who had been in a committed, monogamous relationship for six months with Ursula, a hostess at a tony Malibu restaurant, also wanted to role switch, but in his case, he wanted to go from masculine to feminine in the area of their social calendar.

Leo admitted to Ursula that he really wanted her to tell him things she wanted to do on dates and where she wanted to eat. He was more than willing to pay for their dates, but he wanted her to design them.

At first she felt this change would feel "unromantic," but after a few weeks she found she liked being the "masculine" leader in control of this area. Still, whenever Leo had a good idea, he would tell her, and she would go along with it. They operated with flexibility.

Paul, a television producer, and his girlfriend, Michele, an actress, had been dating for seven months by the time they came into my office.

When they began their relationship, they were both on their best behavior. Michele acted very sexy and adorable and deferred to Paul in most things, and Paul quite naturally cherished Michele's feelings, but because they were both strong, evolved people, both sometimes male and sometimes female, after seven months they had reverted to their natural ways. By the time I saw them, they were in conflict over sharing ideas and feelings.

They collided when he said he wanted one thing and she said she wanted another, or when they both felt bad at the same time and each wanted their feelings cherished by the other. It was clear to me that they could go no further in their relationship, much less negotiate their future, until they learned how to negotiate and compromise through communication.

In their first session I asked, "Who wants to be the male energy and be responsible for leading with ideas, and who wants to be the female energy and support these ideas with feelings?"

A long pause. Then, almost at the same time, they both said that they wanted to be the "male energy" *and* the "female energy."

"In that case," I said, "you are both terminally single and narcissistic, which is fine for people who want to live alone but won't work for couples who want to share their lives together."

I told them that energy is the currency of exchange, and that energy comes either in active maleness or passive femaleness. For a relationship to work, one person must lead with thoughts and the other must "follow" or "respond" with feelings. I advised them both to always be willing to hear the other out without judgment.

Paul and Michele eventually decided that for two weeks he would be the leader and she would follow. I wanted them to experience the roles in harmony, to determine genuine comfort in them.

First, I taught them my "Daily Amigo Talk."

Daily Amigo Talk is a powerful technique to daily vent and stop toxic buildup of unproductive and detrimental emotions like resentment and frustration. It helps avoid denial as a solution to keep the peace.

Each day, whether in person or on the telephone, Paul (as the masculine energy) would say to Michele (the feminine energy), "How do you feel about [*any topic of interest to them*]?" Then, as she answered him, he would listen to her, without interrupting, judging, teaching, or giving suggestions.

After Michele told him her true feelings, Paul would then ask, "What can I do to help you feel better about this?" Michele would tell him, and he would do his best to help her feel better.

Michele (the feminine energy) would then ask Paul (the masculine energy), "What do you think about [*any topic of interest to him*]?" While Paul spoke, Michele listened to him without interrupting, judging, teaching, or giving suggestions.

When Paul was done, Michele would then ask, "What can I do to assist you in achieving this?"

Paul would tell her, and she would do her best to help him.

In the second session, Paul and Michele learned how to deal with their second priority—his feelings and her thoughts.

This is initiated by one person signaling the other that a shift is taking place and then getting the other person to acknowledge a willingness to listen. By doing this, the communication channel switches, but with discipline, not chaos or confusion.

Paul learned how to share his feelings only after saying, "Michele, I have had a bad day," or, "I have some negative feelings I want to share. How do you feel about listening?"

If Michele agreed to listen right then, or acknowledged her willingness to listen at another, more convenient time, he had successfully signaled and gotten permission to talk.

When asking for Michele's permission before dumping his feelings on her, he cherished her feelings above his own, and she then felt respected.

Paul admitted that he often felt challenged by Michele when she told him what she "wanted" from him. I reminded Michele that she must get permission from Paul before sharing ideas, opinions, or suggestions with him. She must ask him if he wants to hear them.

I explained that when she wanted to lead or put out her thoughts or wants, the approach should be, "I have an idea, suggestion, opinion, or want. Are you willing to listen to me now or later?"

By asking Paul's permission to tell him her ideas, she respected him as the leader, which helped him feel cherished by her.

However, if in these negotiations Paul answered with "No, I'm not willing to listen now or later," this would be a red flag, and it would be time for Michele to think about leaving him. But that did not happen.

After experimenting as the masculine energy for two weeks, Michele renegotiated and chose to be the feminine. She did not want a lot of leader responsibility; she just wanted it once in a while.

After a few weeks of practice, Paul and Michele were communicating daily and venting thoughts and feelings smoothly. This enhanced their intimacy enough so that they could bring up all the various "flash points" in their relationship that couples must work out in order to go forward successfully. Negotiating these things before trouble strikes eliminates a lot of stress.

LIVING TOGETHER

One of the biggest issues you will deal with in this phase is: "Should we live together before marriage?"

My warning is: "Don't do it." When you move in with him, you bring your sensuous, sexual self to him without his having to bring you the status of engagement or marriage. He gets a better deal than you do.

Remember, many "shark" men will live with you for your luscious goodies—sex, homemaking skills, companionship— but will resist putting a ring on your finger because, the truth is, what most men want to marry is your virtue. So although a man may talk about the future before you move in, find out what he really means.

What constitutes living together? It means you share the same address. I don't mean "sleeping over." That's *not* living together. Naturally at this stage in your relationship you stay overnight with each other, either at his place or yours, but it's not the same as living together. As long as you (or he) have an "escape" place to go to, you are not "living together," only visiting.

My suggestion is that you not live with a man until you have a ring on your finger—either an engagement ring or a wedding band—or at least until you both have committed to becoming engaged and getting married.

Still, you need to take time *before* moving in together to work out certain issues and avoid painful experiences.

For instance, most masculine men who want to feel in charge require their women to defer to their wishes in the area of logistics. A man may feel uncomfortably out of control at "her place," so it may be appropriate to do "his" or a new "ours."

Since Michele and Paul decided that Paul would be the primary male energy, they decided that she would move into his apartment, which, as it happened, was also larger.

As a professional actress, Michele maintained a large wardrobe for every possible engagement. When Paul and she decided to live together, they needed to look at closets as battlegrounds of the future. Paul, knowing how sensitive Michele was about her wardrobe, needed to not hurt her feelings with blunt logic, such as "Get rid of that old stuff. We don't have space." Instead he needed to say, "We don't have much closet space. What would make you comfortable? Storing your things in a rented space, or getting some wardrobe boxes and putting them in the extra room as if it were a closet?"

In talking in this way, Paul showed that he cared about Michele's feelings, and at the same time, he allowed Michele to relinquish her things on her own, rather than to feel deprived, which would create resentment. Michele ultimately chose to make one small extra bedroom into a closet.

As the masculine-energy-based partner in the relationship, Paul understood that he would always do better with Michele if he cherished her feelings rather than assume she was logical about sensitive issues like treasured clothing.

We women also become upset with men who do not respond sensitively to situations that we feel emotionally about.

"I'm feeling scared about being alone," Michele said to Paul on the telephone one night when he was out of town. "You're okay. The dog is with you. Get some sleep, and I'll talk to you in the morning," Paul said, a rational enough response but one that negated Michele's feelings entirely.

The next week, when they were in therapy, I suggested he would have done better by saying, "I know you're frightened, honey. What do you want me to do?"

Probably, Michele would have said, "It's okay, I just needed to know you cared. I'll be okay. Talk to you tomorrow."

I always ask my audience of women, "How many of you would die for a man who could say, 'Honey, I don't quite get what you're saying. Could you talk more about your feelings?' " If you get a man who says that, tell him what you feel.

A feminine woman would rather have a man say, "This is what I want, how do you feel about it?" than "Would you like this?" or "Would you mind that?" or "Could we do this?"

A man who acts in this way may defend his behavior by saying he wants to be polite, but I believe that a man who doesn't have the courage to say what he wants, risk rejection, and go on with the relationship is not wanting to be a leader. He will manipulate you into leading and then resent you for doing it. So do not allow yourself to be pulled in, unless you want to change your role.

MONEY

Money is an issue you and he have to get to before, not after, you live together because money, like sex, is a potential power-play area. You must have a system agreed upon by both of you or everything will fall apart, either in power games or secret manipulations.

This is a time of the "Open Book," which means you will have a free exchange between you concerning the assets and liabilities of both of you. Even though you may feel uncomfortable with the subject, or reluctant because you're afraid he will think you nosy, you must talk about these issues. Do not just let the sex carry the relationship along.

You need to know if he has ever been in bankruptcy proceedings and what his present credit is like because along with marriage comes the joint sharing of liabilities. As partners in marriage, you are partners in business, and it must be clear what each of you is bringing to the table.

Your masculine-energy man will usually open these issues for discussion by asking you about your debts, rent, car payments, etc. He may even offer to pay them off before marriage—if it is necessary and you cannot pay them immediately—in order to not tarnish his credit. But you can open the discussion by revealing your own financial situation and asking his suggestions about the best way to handle things to secure the best future for you as a couple.

If he doesn't want to talk, you may suspect that something is amiss. Of course, during the second stage, the Imperfect Phase, you might have gotten some clues about his credit if when he took you out to dinner and paid the bill, as his credit card was quietly brought back to your table, he mumbled something like "My secretary didn't send the check out on time."

But that was then, and this is now. Now you are in the third stage, the Negotiable Phase, so you may need to say, "Honey, may I ask you a question about your ideas on how we would handle money if we lived together [engaged or married]?"

If he responds with a flat no with no opening for future talk, he is blocking the discussion, which means trouble deeper than money. It means he does not want to negotiate this issue.

Asking, "What is your reason for not wanting to talk at some time about money?" may get him to tell you any number of things. He may be embarrassed about his credit (you need to know this), or he may be secretive and does not intend to negotiate "his" money, or he just may not be as committed to a future together as you are, and you'd better find that out before you spend a lot of time with him.

Whatever the reason, talking and negotiating in this stage of your relationship will bring success in the fourth stage, which is Commitment. Silence, secretiveness, mind reading, expectations, and assumptions are the qualities of failure. You cannot consider yourself in a marriage-bound relationship until you discuss the issues that are important to you.

Stu, a pilot, had two children by his previous wife. Cassy, a jewelry designer with whom he was now having a serious committed relationship, loved having Stu's children over for visits, but she needed to find out if he was willing to have more children with her.

They had begun talking about marriage after about eight months together, so one day Cassy said, "Stu, what do you think about our having two children if we get married?"

Stu became very quiet and then said, "I'll have to think

about that, Cassy. Four children would be a lot of responsibility for me."

Cassy backed off for a week, and then one day she asked again. She said, "Stu, remember I asked about your thoughts on our having children? Have you got any ideas about it yet?"

Then she held her breath. This was a *big* answer for her. She knew she could not accept a no answer. She would have to leave him, even though she was bonded to him.

"Cassy," Stu said, "I know you want your babies, and you deserve them. The only way I could handle it is if you would be willing either to wait a few years until I could support you all, or if you continue to work part-time, while you had the children. How do you feel about that?"

She was relieved. She needed only to get a yes answer on the children issue. Figuring a way to financially support them was easier. She immediately began to think about something she could do at home to earn money and be with their children.

Stu and Cassy hugged, and Cassy started crying from happiness. It was another successful negotiation for them. They were moving toward total life commitment.

If you and your man are both working, you can share 50-50 if your incomes are nearly equal, or, you can do a percentage amount from both incomes that will cover the household "kitty" and allow each of you leftover money in your separate accounts. Or, you can put away all your combined income in a communal account and draw out stipends, allowances for pin money.

Both of you can pay bills, or you can pay, or he can, or you can alternate months. As long as you have a formula that each is comfortable with, it will work. Having no formula means that one or both of you will try to control with money.

The one rule I support is that the person who brings in the largest portion of money, the masculine "do good to feel good" person, whether man or woman, always has the right to determine whether he or she will control his or her money, allocate control to the spouse, or have a professional do it. Marriage is not an automatic financial turnover situation. The money each person earns is his or hers until turned over to the marriage community. Turning it over must be a free, voluntary, good-business decision.

Women in the past have blindly allowed their husbands to handle money they have earned or inherited as the "right" way. Men also have the right to determine how and who shall control their money in marriage. So you and your man negotiate which of you will handle your finances, overseas investments, retirement plans and budgets and independent allowances for each. It doesn't matter who writes the checks as long as one person is in charge.

There cannot be two presidents in a corporation. In most marriages, the man most often brings in the major money, so usually it is the man who decides how the money is spent, as long as his woman is comfortable. If your ideal is to be the vice president, or the "female," then your man will be the one who structures the finances. As the female energy, you are with a man you respect. You do not compete with him or expect him to be the all-generous daddy to whom you say, "If you loved me, you'd let me do what I want." That's immature and irresponsible.

Of course problems may come along when the equation changes, if children come and one of you stops working, or if both of you are working but resources are stretched and different money priorities emerge, but if you have developed a system of negotiation, you will be able to meet these problems successfully.

I usually tell a feminine-energy woman that her man will feel as comfortable as his career feels. And when he loses his career, or if it is shaky, or his money is mishandled, he gets very ego-shaken.

Michele and Paul worked out a financial arrangement for their future. They agreed that when they got engaged and moved in together, they would each put in 75 percent of their net incomes to cover expenses and leave 25 percent for personal use.

Since Paul presently made more money than Michele did, he would be left with more discretionary money, but she felt comfortable that her contribution was an equitable percentage.

They both acknowledged that due to their professions, the next year could see a reverse—she might be the one making more money.

But if she wasn't, she knew she would have more time to do the book work and account balancing, so she agreed to become the "comptroller" for the couple, promising always to give Paul a monthly profit-and-loss accounting.

PRIVATE PROPERTY

One of the important issues that must be discussed during the Negotiation Phase is how to deal with the equity that either or both of you bring to the relationship.

If he has a lot of money and you don't, does that mean he should use that money to support you? What if you have the money, either through an inheritance or because you are a successful professional woman who has been on her own before meeting this wonderful new man? You may have a substantial investment portfolio, or real estate, art, cars, furniture.

Does that mean that you pay for that trip to Paris that you can afford and he can't? Or that you throw your money and assets into a mutual account, to be drawn on by both?

Well, you can if you want to, but I have found that a man or woman who has worked hard to achieve personal financial security or who has had his or her assets "subdivided" in a previous relationship, often requires a pre- or postnuptial agreement in order to relax about the issue of what will happen to his or her personal assets. The problem is that when the agreement is seen as a battleground, it forecasts danger for the relationship.

What to do? Well, I have found in working with clients who either do have prior money or who are marrying someone with money, that the major negotiation is the prenuptial agreement, which can be positive if both parties understand that it is for security, not stinginess.

If your man requests a prenuptial agreement, my advice is to let him have it. To require a man who has been married before or previously involved in a serious, long-term relationship to go vulnerable again is such a huge risk that he may not marry you unless you can agree.

When Michele and Paul talked about money negotiations, it was he who brought up the idea of a prenuptial agreement. He had inherited a large sum of money.

Michele talked to me about his idea. She asked if there was some sort of agenda behind his not wanting to share with her.

I explained that Paul was justifiably fearful of being vulnerable in this area because of past losses, and that the reality is that life in a relationship can mean weeks, months, or a few years. It usually does not really mean life.

In other words, sometimes love dies. The prenuptial agreement has no effect on the happy lifestyle you create together. It only applies to an unhappy relationship that needs to be fairly terminated.

I explained to Michele that if and when the time came to sign the contract, instead of fighting Paul, she should take the document to her attorney to determine if she was being dealt with fairly.

However, if she rebelled against the very idea of an agreement, Paul would probably question the integrity of Michele's motives, and thereby intensify the situation and suspect that Michele was looking toward a divorce with "gain."

By the way, Michele did take Paul's prenuptial agreement to her attorney, who saw only one thing that he would have her ask for, and that was that if the marriage was going fine, the prenuptial agreement would be set aside in five years.

Paul agreed, and his fears were alleviated. It was a healthy and productive compromise in which they both felt comfortable.

SPACE, MAINTENANCE, AND CHORES

Unless you and your mate are a "perfect match," which, by the way, never happens, you must talk about such things as space, maintenance, and chores before anyone starts packing or unpacking. You must feel secure about how things will be laid out in these areas, so as to avoid problems later.

By private space, I mean rooms, closets, and drawers. Maintenance, on the other hand, refers to the plumbing and heating; the chores to doing the dishes, the laundry, taking care of the car—and all of these responsibilities need to be sorted out. Who will wait for the telephone repairman? Who does the shopping? Cooking? Cleaning?

Many women—and men—make the mistake of thinking that chores are allocated by gender, but there are no gender-related tasks; there are only physical limitations due to height, weight, and dexterity.

In addition, some men like to grocery-shop, either because they enjoy doing it and like to cook, or because it gives them a way of controlling the spending. Maybe they're into coupon clipping (men love bargains). Some women have no patience for grocery shopping at all. It's all a matter of negotiating the division of labor. You do it better, or it's more important to you, so you take it over.

Some men love housekeeping, and some women love carpentry. I suggest that you sit down with your man and make a list of household responsibilities, then choose how to delegate them between you equitably. Open negotiations, with no one "giving in" resentfully, will allow a couple to live together peacefully.

What I want you to do is to have an agenda (for time, space, money, and play) and deliberately go over each item with your man until a good contract is built. Then you must redo this agreement regularly, as needed.

Gwen and Steve didn't know any of this, until they experienced it firsthand.

"Will you move in with me?" Steve asked Gwen one night after they had been dating for about six months. They re-met after a Kenosha High School reunion and found out that each was now living in Los Angeles, she a flight attendant and he an associate at a major law firm.

They began dating, and the pleasure they found in being together was a source of surprise and joy to them both. It was sustained by their shared memories and hometown experiences and by their growing compatibility and deepening feelings for each other.

Then the lease on Steve's apartment ran out, and he and Gwen talked about his moving into her apartment. It seemed logical because they had begun to talk in earnest about becoming engaged and then leasing or buying a place together.

But the problems began almost immediately after he moved in. She was neat, and he was sloppy. Steve would leave his clothes on the chair in their bedroom. Gwen would dutifully put away his clothes, and then act her best martyr role until his guilt would take over and he would comply with her wishes, that is, until the next time. Gwen became angry that he didn't change to please her.

Whenever they fought, Gwen would move into "her" extra room, which would leave Steve feeling rejected, until he could cajole her back into "their" room. If he couldn't get her to come back to "their" room, he would storm out and head straight for a neighborhood bar where he would pour out his troubles to the friendly bartender.

Meanwhile, she hated the amount of time he spent in front of his computer and felt rejected. In fact, both of them felt rejected by the other, and each denied vehemently that he or she was doing the rejecting.

Then there was the problem of money. Gwen was reluctant to begin saving money toward purchasing their house. She wanted to keep her money for her needs and let him buy the house, but Steve was not that old-fashioned. He wanted equitable sharing.

Naturally, the friction had an impact on their sex life.

Soon both Steve and Gwen began to wonder if they had done the right thing in living together. They became confused and fearful about planning the future. Hearing about me from a mutual friend, they made an appointment to come to my office.

MUTATE, DON'T ELIMINATE

At this point, both Gwen and Steve understood that real life was encroaching on their otherwise romantic courtship, and although each could have picked up his or her marbles and moved on, I did urge them and would urge anyone encountering or butting reality to stay and dig in.

I don't believe in divorce—legal or emotional—as long as there is any piece of love left. Love is so hard to come by that when you do get a little of it, you should nurture it to the very end.

As I said earlier, I feel that if you get someone who is, maybe, 51 percent or above, keep that person. That is to say, if you like more about the person than you don't, then keep him, because the odds are that if you don't and go out looking for a better deal, you could end up with someone who is 49 percent or worse.

So don't abort a relationship that has value in it. Stay until you cannot stay. You will know the time to leave because you will feel both empathetic and apathetic toward your mate. The spark and the angry feelings will be gone.

I often say, "She who leaves first in anger is doomed to repeat the relationship experience. She who stays until the end when the lessons are learned moves to the next step in relationship skills."

Gwen and Steve did decide to stay, and it was in this period that they learned to negotiate a deal that allowed each of them the freedom to be themselves while sharing the responsibilities of the relationship. One of the things they needed to recognize was that it was problems and crises that stimulated them to start negotiating. They needed to learn to talk about issues before they turned into problems.

Because Steve moved in with *her*, Gwen had a lot of masculine power in doing what she wanted. The resulting problem was Gwen's unwillingness to talk through issues. Instead, she ran off to her own room, thereby eliminating Steve until he reacted to her leaving by leaving himself.

Steve wanted to be the masculine to her feminine. He eventually solved this problem by not leaving but going into her "private" room and confronting the issue. The result was that they both committed to talk at least fifteen minutes once a day about resentments and appreciations of each other. I call this *"we* time." This was the beginning of an "Amigo Talk System," rather than just running away to be alone (*"I* time"). After negotiation, Gwen allowed herself to let go of her masculine side in deference to Steven's.

There are three systems of dealing with your partner: You can intimidate him with fear, you can seduce him with guilt, or you can negotiate with love, remembering that love is acceptance. Gwen and Steve had been dealing through guilt and fear. When Gwen began hibernating in her room, she was trying to make Steve feel guilty, and when Steve began leaving the apartment, he was trying to frighten her.

By reassessing their relationship through my negotiation methods, using love, they learned to accommodate their individual needs.

Soon Gwen's standard of homemaking was respected by Steve, his leadership in finances was respected by her, and her being in charge of the social calendar dates and interior design was respected by him. As they lived with their commitments, they continued to negotiate readjustments rather than fight.

If a man thinks of his living space simply as a place where he gets gratified, where he can sit, where his woman "mothers" him and he doesn't have to take her out on a date or bring people into the relationship, then he is going to dry her up, because she needs to feel good, she needs to get out there, and she needs to have some fun in her life with him.

It is a masculine man's job to give that pleasure to her or risk losing her. It is a feminine woman's job to appreciate his efforts and respond joyfully.

TIME

Although in the first hot days of a romance you and he cannot get enough of each other, once a relationship is established and real life enters the picture, each of you has different ideas about the way you expect to spend your time. Sometimes you want to be with your mate and sometimes not. This is the time that both partners have to negotiate to learn how to integrate their past and present lives and selves.

I suggest that dating alone, as a couple, at least once a week is important to keep the romance alive, and that socializing at least twice a month with people each of you finds interesting will gradually build a pool of friends both enjoy.

You had friends, relatives, hobbies, and sports in your life before you met your new love interest. For a relationship to be healthy, it must add to your private life, not detract. In order to incorporate your past into your present, you must negotiate an overall agreement for the time you spend alone and together.

Ben, an oral surgeon, was more dependent on his girlfriend, Lois, a high-powered TV executive, than she liked. "He seems needy, clingy," she said. "It turns me off."

"She's too independent," Ben said. "I want us to be more centered on being a couple than on being individuals. Isn't that what a relationship is?"

"No," I answered. "In order to be a good 'we,' you both must stand alone as individual 'I' 's. Don't forget to be 'I' in favor of 'we,' or you will ruin everything."

PLAY

When Aaron and his girlfriend, Tina, played, they had lots of fun. Aaron was a member of a rowing crew, and he raced with his team as often as he could; he also played golf once a week. Tina loved to play tennis, and she enjoyed being a spectator at Aaron's rowing matches. They supported each other's personal hobbies.

As far as their time together was concerned, they enjoyed plays and movies, especially screenings, since these were valuable for their careers (they were both actors). They also enjoyed entertaining at home and traveling. Aaron and Tina were compatible in enough areas to be able to share their playtime, alone and together.

But things were more problematic for Diane and Joel, who at one counseling session talked about their upcoming vacation plans. Joel, an insurance agent, wanted to spend their two-week vacation together bicycle-touring New England, whereas Diane, a dancer, wanted to rent a cottage on Cape Cod and take smaller biking excursions on day trips. Obviously, they both liked vacationing in New England and bicycling. Their only conflict was a set location or multiple ones.

Usually, or at least since they had been coming to see me, Diane, who was the feminine energy in the relationship, would deliberately defer to Joel and respect his thinking ahead of her own. However, going on vacation seemed like a "feeling" issue to Diane. She believed her feelings deserved to be cherished above his logic. They were both angry and ready to end their vacation plans, and maybe their relationship of eight months.

The question was, how to achieve a win-win instead of a win-lose situation? In order to resolve it, we needed to know what Joel thought and why.

Joel's logic told him that variety was more important than stability. "I don't want to be stuck in one place," he said. "I don't get to that part of the country that often, and I want to see as much as I can." Clearly, he wanted Diane to defer to him.

She wanted the same. Diane wanted to get to know a specific area and to have time to just be together, to relax and unwind from the pressures of their lives. The issue seemed so equal—he wanted respect; she wanted to be cherished.

My advice: Compromise for best results.

Joel agreed to one location (the cottage) for this trip, since it was a fun, feeling vacation, not a decathlon training program for bicyclers, and Diane promised that their next trip would be a bike tour through some other parts of New England. Once they "got off" on winning, they stopped losing.

SEXUAL NEGOTIATIONS

Since sex is a Pandora's box that can stop a relationship cold, I will devote the next few chapters to this subject. However, here I will say that when it is time to negotiate sexual issues, do it while sitting or standing upright. *You don't negotiate sexual issues lying down.* It is too vulnerable an issue at a time of intimacy. The pain would be compounded.

By the way, you do not tell your man how many other men you have slept with or how good in bed they were. The only things from the past you need to "confess" are venereal or other diseases that could impact on the other's well-being. In some states, you can be arrested for keeping such health secrets.

Regularly (monthly in the first year, bimonthly in the second, and at least every three months till death or divorce), talk about time, space, money, and play. Renegotiate if it is necessary.

CHAPTER 15

How to Have Sex and Make It Great

We have just come out of an era of instant gratification (the eighties), and most of us are now realizing (perhaps initiated by the AIDS crisis) that real lovemaking is more satisfying than indiscriminate sex. To have a meaningful and lasting relationship, we must go from shallow, dangerous, polygamous sex games into satisfying, monogamous lovemaking.

How do you get satisfying lovemaking? By having good chemistry together, by sharing a compatible lifestyle, and by communicating all of this to each other verbally. And, finally, by agreeing to a commitment of monogamy, continuity, and longevity.

If one or both of you is interested only in passionate sex without a committed relationship, then you both need to be aware of this. That way you can agree that what you are about to embark on is not intended to be a committed, marriage-bound relationship. No matter what your individual goals are, you must discuss them before sex, or one of you may be hurt.

If you can speak the truth to one another, sex then becomes "making love," a time of intimacy, trust, and caring, and the pitfalls of shallow, anonymous gratification are avoided. Verbal communication lays the groundwork for free and erotic lovemaking in which each person knows the other is a real human and not a projection of his or her fantasy.

If you want the best sexual, lovemaking experience, first deal with these questions.

1. Why do I want sexual intimacy with this person?
2. Will this encounter make me feel desirable?
3. What is the long-term goal for this encounter?
4. Am I seeking vengeance against men?
5. Do I like this person, or am I just using him?
6. Is the drink, pill, snort, having sex, or am I?

WHO'S ON TOP?

It is in nature alone that anatomy is destiny, because nature requires that a male sperm chase the female egg, which allows only one sperm to enter after a long, hard fight against the odds. But in human beings, there is a choice. The only requirement for a successful sexual union is that the two people be of opposite energy, no matter what their gender. One person must be the passionate, active, masculine pursuer, and the other the affectionate, receptive, feminine one who is pursued. So, although each person in a relationship is unique in his or her sexual needs, each must know his or her preference and priorities. If you and your man are too similar in style, you will have problems.

For example, if you are both the passionate, active, masculine pursuer, you will certainly, like Leslie and Mark, get it on ASAP, but you may not become well enough acquainted before sex to know if you have chosen a compatible life partner. If you are both affectionate, passive, and receptive, little action will take place. Each person will wait for the other to make the approach.

But choosing your primary role does not mean that is a lifetime commitment. Later, when you are a committed couple, you can add variety for spice. You may go from male giving to female receiving. This is fine, too, as long as you negotiate these changes with your partner.

The two things to decide before you have sex are whether

you are the male or the female energy, and whether sex only is what you want or making love is your goal. If you are interested in making love, and not just having casual sex, you must *first* find out if your partner wants the same.

SEX WITHOUT LOVE

If you have chosen to be the feminine, receiving energy, you must, for safety's sake, be in control of who makes love to you so you can feel safe and open. It is the receiver who has the veto, or "no" right, which is where *all* the sexual power resides. Sperm is cheap; eggs are precious. The feminine receiver must be "cherished" in order for great sex to occur.

Although most masculine-energy-based men want sexual release of tension through ejaculation, most feminine-energy-based women do not want sex unless it fulfills some emotional need.

When a woman allows herself or is forced to become sexual without love, her self-esteem drops, and she helplessly believes she is not lovable or desirable to good men. With little self-esteem, she often compulsively seeks validation through more promiscuous sexual contacts, believing that "giving" good sex will help her keep her man. It doesn't.

Remember Leslie and Mark? When Mark withheld sexual contact, Leslie found herself sexualizing food. It became her love object. Mark, on the other hand, could use the bodies of women as useful objects when he needed strokes. The old saying goes, "Men give love to get sex; women give sex to keep this love."

Of course, there are men who are "feminine," who give sex to get and keep love, and there are women who are "masculine," who give love to get sex. Which are you?

THE TWO KINDS OF SEXUALITY

I call one kind of sexuality masculine "staircase" sex, and the other feminine "wheel" sex.

Feminine "wheel" sex is preferred by "feminine" women or men who tend to be relationship-oriented. They are not in it basically for the physical gratification. The feminine person needs sensitive, emotional support around the sexual act. Her sexuality is more like a "wheel" in which every action in the relationship impacts on her sexual experience. The person who is the female sexual energy will be greatly affected by emotional exchanges between the two people during the day. The tone of "his" voice during a phone conversation, whether he was late and why, the look on his face, whether he seemed bored at dinner in the restaurant and eager to run home for sex, all the things that happen between the two people *before* getting into bed affect the way the feminine man or woman responds to his or her partner sexually.

But the masculine sex drive is little affected by extraneous happenings during the day. If he basically feels respected in the relationship, little about the day gets in the way of his sex drive. It moves straight ahead, directed toward orgasm and release.

Patrice, a floral designer, was a very romantic and feminine woman who was in a committed relationship with Nick, a charismatic and dynamic businessman, who in the first three months of their relationship had been wonderfully romantic, prompt for dates, always remembering to call if he was going to be late, bringing surprise gifts, flowers, and cute cards. He was always very affectionate.

But by the fourth month, Patrice noticed a laxness creeping into their romance. Nick was often late and seldom bothered to call to let her know of his change in plans.

Patrice told Nick that this behavior was unsettling to her, but each time she spoke to him, he'd shrug off her words. He would reply, "Okay, but I'm here now, so let's drop it."

Soon the little gifts and flowers became less frequent, until they stopped entirely except on her birthday or special holidays. Then he began to criticize small things that Patrice did. Still, regardless of how the day went between them, Nick wanted to make love each time they saw each other. But Patrice was very much influenced by the "little things" and soon became unresponsive to the sexual act with him. She began to feel more like an object of his sexual release than the cherished woman in his life. These feelings were not communicated between them, and as a result Patrice became depressed over the situation.

When Patrice told me of her problem at one of my seminars, my advice was that she pick a quiet, peaceful time and ask Nick if he would listen to some feelings she'd been holding in that were troubling her.

If he said yes, I advised her to then tell him that she loved those little things he used to do—his flowers, warm phone calls, those small romantic gestures that made her feel sexually responsive. She must also tell him about the things he did that closed her up to sex with him—his tardiness, careless words of criticism, lack of compliments or appreciation, his breezy affection without involvement. She was to tell him that one negative thing, which might seem like nothing to him, could prevent her from responding totally.

I suggested she present these things not as a command, but rather as a sharing of her feelings.

Patrice did share with Nick her need and desire for romance before turning on to him. Nick was very responsive and felt foolish and regretful that he had been so careless and unaware.

Having penetrating, controlling, passionate intercourse is very male in energy. Making total love, physically, mentally, and emotionally, is very feminine and affection-based.

Feminine, receptive women and men are "horny" for lovemaking, and not just intercourse. That is, they don't initiate intercourse, but rather initiate affection. And when they receive affectionate foreplay during the day and in bed, they turn on and give back passionate intercourse. "Slam-bam, thank you, ma'am" is for masculine people, whether male or female. Slow and easy is for feminine people, whether female or male.

Wheel sex fulfills a feminine woman or man's need to be cherished in foreplay. It involves affection, touching, feeling, ambling its way to intercourse, all flowing together as part of a continuum. When a man understands the concept of wheel sex and practices it, he will not only help his receptive woman feel cherished, but he will get greater pleasure because he is giving greater pleasure to his receptive woman.

Laurie, a successful real estate broker, was the girlfriend of Ben, the owner of a restaurant and a typical big "I" gamesman. Ben would make love to Laurie with well-determined perfunctory touches, grabs, and kisses, in supposedly erotic zones for a woman.

For Ben, this kind of sex was fine. It was the way he'd always done it. He was well-meaning, but clearly he had no clue as to how to make love to a woman and satisfy her. So their loving would result in his orgasm but not hers, leaving her silent, frustrated, and angry.

Of course, Laurie, who was no fool, knew what good sex could be like with the right man. She loved Ben and believed he loved her, too, but the relationship was beginning to strain. So how was she to convey her desire to rescript their pattern of lovemaking without humiliating him or compromising her role in the relationship as a feminine woman?

Laurie needed to communicate with Ben in a way that he could hear and learn from. She chose to ask him if she could talk to him, at his convenience, about their sexual relationship.

Ben agreed nervously, fearing her criticisms. He knew she was not sexually satisfied, but he also knew he didn't know a better way. He had read books about making love to a woman and followed formulas he had read, but they didn't work with Laurie.

"Ben, I know you love me and are trying to please me, and I appreciate you for it. However, I like certain things to happen that really turn me on. Are you willing to learn what they are?"

Ben was relieved that she was going to tell him what pleased her instead of telling him what he had done wrong. They crawled into bed and under the covers like kids playing. She slowly showed him how she liked to be touched and where by guiding his hands. She whispered the things she liked to happen to her body in his ear until he could not stop from making love to her on the spot.

This time it was different, because she could maneuver his hands and body with hers, because he wanted her to. She could verbalize her desires because he had told her that she could. She was not a demanding mother with a bad boy. She was a woman whose man *wanted* her to teach him how to be her lover. And he was still the respected man and she the cherished woman.

Ben began making love to Laurie leisurely and with attention to find her special erotic little pleasure zones. For the first time in their relationship, Laurie began to respond voluptuously to her man, and Ben's reward was not only his awareness of the great orgasm and immense pleasure he was giving his woman, but his own deeper orgasm, much better in every way than the ones he previously had with his mechanical, awkward, and unsatisfying gestures toward this woman he truly loved and wanted to please.

For Jane and George, who were both musicians in their early twenties, the problem was George's sexual inhibitions and inexperience with women. Jane, a strong, dynamic, masculine-energy woman, loved her George's gentle touches. She enjoyed his smoothing her hair, gliding his hands over her skin, giving secret kisses, and making love tenderly, but she also wanted more passionate sex.

Since they had just committed to one another, their sexual relationship was new, and the truth was that George was not fulfilling her needs. He did not spontaneously and lustfully enjoy himself or her body. She knew he had passion within because it would break out periodically while making love, but it would just as quickly go underground.

Jane wanted to make the relationship work, but she wanted good sex too. She feared George would close down completely if she talked negatively about her problem.

She came to see me, and I suggested she use direct physical means to loosen up George's natural passion. It would be up to her to lead him to the kind of sexuality she wanted, since she was the masculine pursuer.

Jane invited George to her place for dinner and met him at the door in a sensuous silk lounging gown (not a threatening erotic teddy). All the romantic maneuvers were in place, dim lights, candles, soft music, a glass of wine, a light meal, a request to slow-dance, her undressing him, a bath together with lots of sudsy touching, followed by a fabulous and erotic massage.

As she rubbed him, Jane talked about some of her sexual fantasies. She pursued him sensuously until he was so turned on he could not help but be passionate with her. Then, later in bed, he was so turned on by turning her on, they had the first of many wonderful sexual experiences in which both were fulfilled.

It is important to let your masculine man know how wonderful it feels to you when he plays the wheel of your senses: touching, tasting, smelling, seeing, and hearing, on the way to intercourse and orgasm. This will give you greater pleasure because you will feel cherished as a human being and not an object to be used.

Another way your man can bring you pleasure and get wonderful results is by talking affectionately to you. I call it "Sweet Talk," and feminine-energy sex partners love Sweet Talk because they fall in love through their ears, while male-energized men and women fall in love through their eyes.

The way you talk to your man is of utmost importance. Patrice talked politely and not critically to Nick about his mistakes. Criticizing a masculine man can cause him so much inner pain that he cannot hear what you are saying and will often react defensively or run away.

Feminine Laurie got verbal permission to teach masculine Ben how she liked sex. She also was gentle about Ben's inner (feminine) feelings, not critical like an authority-figure "Mom."

If you are the feminine energy who chooses to be cherished, you need to protect *your* sexual feelings, not *his*. Doing nothing when sex is not bringing you pleasure means it will go on indefinitely. It will cause not only feelings of being taken for granted, but resentment, frustration, and anger, which can be damaging to your relationship. You will best do this just as Patrice and Laurie did—by asking permission to share your feelings.

If he won't talk, leave him. It means he is too selfish to be with. If he listens, speak "I feel" statements, not "you are wrong" statements. Especially tell him what you don't want, i.e., uncommitted sex, polygamy, rough sex, and "slam-bam, thank you, ma'am" sex.

However, speak to him like a polite human being, not an emotional, judgmental hysteric. He cannot hear or learn from you when you act irrationally, even if, out of love for you, he accepts your doing it this way.

Remember, most masculine men will not change unless required to do so. As a feminine person, you must communicate your negative feelings about a sexual relationship that is void of romantic spice.

THE PAST REVISITED—SEX PROBLEMS

We all carry "baggage" from our past into our sexual relationships. Possibly we have been miseducated, inhibited by religious training, abandoned, or, most often, still plagued with painful memories of rejection by a previous lover. All of these things tend to plant false ideas in our minds, which damage us sexually and make us wary of future encounters.

This is a natural but self-defeating and destructive process, because when we bring ignorance, hurts, and disappointments into the next man's bed, it can subvert our natural, healthy sexuality.

We must work hard to free ourselves of these ghosts in the bedroom and begin to make sexual decisions that are our own and not someone else's. Unless we change our false beliefs, the damage will show up in our new relationships, even before we attempt to be sexual.

Following are seven common faulty premises that women hold and some new ways to think and act in order to defuse these issues and help your new relationship off to a good start.

FAULTY PREMISE 1
"IF I GIVE A MAN SEX, HE WILL GIVE ME BACK A COMMITMENT."

Wrong! Masculine men do not "give back" a commitment for free sex. Masculine men know that there are no free lunches, and what appears to be "free sex" usually has strings attached—the strings being a woman who says, "Marry me," or "I'm pregnant," or "I feel used." So smart, "taker" men get the sex free and then run away without paying, leaving a woman bonded and in pain.

Masculine men give commitments when they are required to, by women who don't "need" a man but prefer one in order to add to their already functioning lives. Don't "give back" sex until you negotiate the "give back" commitment from him. Buyer beware!

By the way, if you are a woman who chooses to be the masculine energy, please practice sexual integrity with the men you pursue sexually. Sensitive, feminine-energy-based men do "give back" sex and commitment to strong, masculine women who pursue them by giving them sex, money, and status. Most men, whether feminine or masculine, logically believe in their ability to think clearly, so they risk a great deal when they find they have been "used" as "sex machines" by unscrupulous women. This thoroughly undermines their feeling of adequacy.

Feminine women who become aware of their being abused feel undesirable and unlovable, and often resort to bingeing on food, drink, drugs, or casual sex to mask their pain.

FAULTY PREMISE 2
"SEXUAL VIRTUE IS PASSÉ."

Wrong! Men don't fall in love with your vagina, no matter how great a sex partner you are. They may fall into sex addiction, but they will not fall in love, which, by definition, must be with the total you—mind, body, and spirit.

Historically, parents, churches, and culture have attempted

to teach virtue, but with the advent of the birth control pill, the sexual revolution, and the women's movement, these precepts seemed outdated. The result was that society rebelled against virtue and began to indulge in spontaneous casual sex, only to rue the day after.

I believe that virtue is synonymous with personal integrity, with how honest we are to ourselves. A man or woman who honestly says, "I am not interested in a committed relationship. I only want some fun," has, to my way of thinking, integrity but not spiritual virtue.

The man (or woman) who acts seductively and suggests the possibility of a committed relationship in order to get sex lacks integrity and virtue as well. These people are dangerous. They sexually "use" gentle women (or men), who, once burned, may then themselves become cynical users of others.

Your intuition will tell you who the "users" are. Don't ignore that little voice inside of you that says, "Something is wrong here. I don't feel right." My advice is either get a commitment or get away.

FAULTY PREMISE 3
"CASUAL SEX IS A GOOD WAY TO GET TO KNOW SOMEONE."

Wrong! Casual sex is a way to lower the anxiety of anticipation. The anticipation of romance, union, and completion can be so painful that "getting it over with" becomes more important than intimacy, slowly and carefully built.

Is sex the bloom or the roots of a relationship? I believe that sex is the bloom, not the roots. The roots must be planted deep into compatibility, communication, and friendship. When the relationship grows out of sex, it can become an addiction between incompatible, uncommunicative, unfriendly people who need the sex hit, not the intimacy. But when sex is the bloom, and the roots are grounded in true human, erotic love, it can last through the peaks and valleys of life.

FAULTY PREMISE 4
"ALL I NEED TO DO IS HAVE MEDICALLY SAFE SEX."

It is true that medically safe sex is the beginning of security, but it is not enough. In a relationship, sensitive women and men also need emotionally safe sex, grounded in their being known for who they are and heard for what they want.

It is not uncommon for women who try to resist casual sex to find themselves either seduced ("I'll give you a commitment *someday*, but not today!") or intimidated ("You're not being fair to me," or "You're lucky to have me!") by someone trying to talk them into sex. Being hostage to a controlling person can be as dangerous as having unsafe sex. The time and energy it takes to withdraw and heal from a bad deal can be just as destructive as many sexually transmitted diseases. AIDS can kill the body, but so can depression. Taking an AIDS test and taking time to know the other person and have him or her know you work best together for safety.

FAULTY PREMISE 5
"I CAN 'FIX' MY PARTNER'S SEX PROBLEMS."

Sex problems are, along with financial problems, one of the most obvious symptoms of inner turmoil. It is grandiose and presumptuous to assume that you can "fix" someone's sex problems. You can work with a partner (or a client, if you are a therapist), but you cannot fix her or his problems.

Each of us must identify our problems and commit to rehabilitation, although we can draw upon the aids of therapy and self-help books or groups. But no one can be fixed from outside. It is an inside job. Dysfunctional people often like to believe their sex problems can be "fixed" from the outside. Needy people often like to be needed. These two people meet—the fixer (one who believes that he or she can teach the other how to be functional) and the one who needs to be fixed, and the game is on.

If you want to accept a sexually dysfunctional person as is, do it, but don't "hope" for a change. If you do not want to commit to a dysfunctional person, reject him or her as soon as possible, mercifully. Don't tolerate dysfunction, or you will become dysfunctional yourself. Grandiose fixers and tyrannical victims somehow deserve each other. Choose carefully.

If you want to be a sex therapist, get a license. If you want a good marriage, get a good lover. We live too long to be sexually frustrated and unfulfilled.

FAULTY PREMISE 6
"ONCE I AM IN A COMMITTED RELATIONSHIP, I DON'T HAVE TO CONTINUE MY SEXUAL COURTSHIP STYLE."

Wrong! When one person switches sexual courtship styles (without negotiation) in midrelationship, it can be very threatening to the other person. Most women are turned off when their aggressive, masculine-style man suddenly turns passive in bed.

But it is not only women who turn off. Sexual aversion and impotence are becoming major problems for men these days. They are turning off sexually to narcissistic women who want to be respected for their ideas and also cherished for their feelings. Men who turn off don't want to be a drone to a queen bee, so they sexually shut down as their way to not cherish her with sexual pleasure.

Some men like to lead, and some men don't. With women's rights being promoted, men's rights to determine whom they want or don't want sex with are being confronted.

FAULTY PREMISE 7
"MASCULINE MEN LIKE WOMEN WHO SHARE SEXUAL INITIATING RESPONSIBILITIES EQUALLY."

Wrong! Most masculine men do not like sexual initiating responsibilities to be shared. They want to be the sexual aggressors, and they want their feminine women to respond and give back.

Does that mean that if you are a feminine woman, you can't initiate sex when you are in the mood? It might, because becoming a couple means compromising some of your rights and freedoms as an individual for the benefit of the relationship.

However, most healthy men and women will be able to share "equitably" in the sexual area if they can negotiate their preferences. The challenge for romantic partners is to compassionately and truthfully talk about sexual styles and be sensitively aware of the other's feelings.

I suggest that if you are a feminine woman who wants to initiate sex with your committed partner, you say, "Fred, sometimes I look at you and just want to start making love right then. Would it turn you off if I approached you like that?"

Of course, narcissistic men and women, who want their sexual desires respected and their sensitive feelings cherished, cannot be negotiated with because when their partner tries to initiate his or her own sexual wants, they feel challenged, and the competition begins. These men and women intimidate and/or seduce to get their own way and accuse their partners of destroying the relationship with their negativity (saying no) and selfishness.

Too often sensitive, sensuous, sexual men and women who don't like to fight will shut down and ignore their own sexual needs in deference to the narcissistic partner, hoping things will change equitably. They never do.

A TECHNIQUE FOR UNDOING SEXUAL DAMAGE

Sexuality is the bonding element in a relationship. Your last sensual/sexual experience forms the basis of pleasure for your next experience.

When sexual memories of the last encounter are good, it forms the baseline foundation for the next encounter. When negative memories are formed, especially for men, sexual aversion or stalemate follows, and they fall out of love.

Robin, an attractive cosmetologist, spoke to me after a seminar about her boyfriend, John, a handsome construction worker a few years older than she, with whom she was building a solid, loving relationship. Their only problem, she told me, was their sex life, which had inexplicably taken a turn for the worse.

John was working long, hard hours on a housing project, and when he came over to see her in the evenings, he would make perfunctory love to her, totally unlike the great sex they'd had before.

When Robin tried to bring up her sexual dissatisfaction, John would counter with, "Look, Robin, I'm working like a crazy man. I'm tired. I'm stressed out. I've got problems with this job. What do you expect? I'm exhausted!"

Robin asked me what to do, and I suggested my technique of sensate focusing. I have found that this helps couples to develop the art of making love.

Sensate Focusing Exercises

1. Set aside at least two hours, when no interruptions will occur, either at home or at a hotel, in a bathtub or hot tub or Jacuzzi that can hold two people.
2. Lock doors; disconnect phones and beepers.
3. *Don't talk at all* during these two hours. Only body language can be used. Talk is a left-lobe, intellectual activity. Making love is a right-lobe, nonverbal activity.
4. The "male"-energy person will bring:
    Finger foods for each to feed the other
    A tape or record or sensuous music without vocals
    Candles and incense
    Writing paper and pens or pencils
    Powder or oil

Instructions:

Feed, wash, dry, oil, powder, massage each other and have sex or don't, depending on "male" desire, "female" availability, and sleep or rest. *Don't talk* from the beginning of the encounter until the end. Use candles (turn off all electric lights), music, and incense. Signal pleasure and discomfort physically, but not verbally.

After the bath and massage, write a letter to the other about the experience, exchange the letters, and write a response back. Exchange your responses, and then talk.

This exercise will enhance your pleasure or intensify your painful fear of intimacy. If this fear cannot be alleviated in a few bathing sessions, seek help from therapy. Make certain the therapist is certified as a sex therapist.

This nonverbal, sensuous focusing exercise is designed to help bodies re-bond chemically. Bodies "forget" each other and de-bond if neglected. Workaholics and distracted men and women forget to taste, touch, smell, see, and hear each other often enough to remember the pleasure.

Robin told John about this exercise, and although at first he laughed nervously at the idea of contrived sex, he finally gave in, and after one romantic evening in which Robin brought the candles, munchies, music, and massage oil and kept silent in their bath together, he never balked again.

John liked the relaxation in a hot bath for his tired body, and he also liked not having to talk. Robin liked the slow washing, drying, and massaging.

Robin and John found a new way to make love that fulfilled both their needs, and, in fact, after that John became the initiator of these special times together, and their sex life resumed full blast.

This exercise may seem clumsy at first, contrived or artificial, until you feel the pleasure. Hopefully, you will enjoy the experience so much you will want to do it for yourselves, not just because it is a helpful technique.

MALE SEXUAL DYSFUNCTION

The exercise I just suggested is also good to use if your man has a problem with premature ejaculation or impotence. Male sexual dysfunction may have a physical or psychological base. I shall deal only with the psychological issue here, since the medical is out of my field of competency as a marriage and family counselor.

SEMINAL RETENTION

Although some men can control their orgasm deliberately in order to extend their sexual activity longer, thus enjoying themselves and the pleasure they can give, others suffer from psychological dysfunctional seminal retention, or the inability to release into orgasm. These are men who can achieve an erection and can give their partner pleasure but cannot let go of themselves enough to achieve orgasm. Psychologists have suggested that this not-uncommon problem is based on a fear of being vulnerable and committed.

If your partner appears to be suffering from an inability to achieve an orgasm, you can greatly enhance your lovemaking by an attitude of acceptance, of unconditional love. Criticizing, teasing, or demanding only deepens the fear and causes more problems. In order for a man who is the giver to perform well, he must be with a feminine woman who receives well and is not judgmental.

Seminal retention can sometimes be a very loving technique by a man in order to maintain "staying power" for lovemaking. The Chinese advise men to give one hundred orgasms to a woman before releasing themselves. This ideal may not be realistic, but the intent is wonderful. Tantric yoga also stresses sensuality over sexual gratification. The mind, not the body, is the seat of good sex. Using self-discipline and control to enhance sexual intimacy is what turns sex into lovemaking.

IMPOTENCE

In working with single men in relationships, I have found that impotence is often a fear-based dysfunction.

The modern, self-actualized woman can sometimes be a bit

too much for a masculine, right-handed man. One minute she is assertive/aggressive, the next she is passive. In the absence of female behavior that is logical or predictable, the man, like the Pavlovian dog, can eventually lose his potency on all levels. Depression in men often looks like passive-aggressive behavior. "He could do it if he wanted to," she says.

In truth, he has shut down out of self-preservation. He will sometimes "check out the machinery" with less threatening women and find his impotency is not with all women, only with a woman who frightens him.

I advise women to pick their style of sexuality, either active-assertive or passive-receptive, and stay with it, in order to avoid "training" their man to be impotent.

But what if you want to change your sexual style? How do you do that without causing him to become impotent? The best way to avoid a bad sexual reaction in a man or a woman is to *talk*.

But once again, the problem that evolved people have is that they speak from both sides of their brain. They talk about both their thoughts and their feelings, which results in confusion.

So a woman must pick her style, either masculine, i.e., "I think, I want, my opinion is, please respect me, and I will cherish you for doing it," or feminine, i.e., "I feel good, confused, stifled, neglected, please cherish me, and I will respect you for doing it."

No matter what the sexual subject is—AIDS testing, birth control, dysfunctions, fantasies—speak from your side of the relationship.

If you have chosen to be female, say, "I would really *enjoy* having one of your massages." If you have chosen to be male, say, "I *think* it would be fun to make love in the Jacuzzi." That way the other person can now "hear" you and "know" where you are coming from and respond either by saying, "That sounds like fun to me, too," if you are the feminine energy, or "I can do that, honey," if you are the masculine.

PREMATURE EJACULATION

Sometimes a man suffers from "premature ejaculation" when he is selfish and doesn't care about a woman's need to be made love to affectionately. I call this malady "deficient affectionate lovemaking."

But sometimes premature ejaculation on the part of the man can be traced directly to the actions of his woman. For example, when a woman is being hypercritical, i.e., "Don't touch me that way," "Don't mess my hair," or "I hope you can hold off this time until I am satisfied," he will be too tense to enjoy lovemaking and will get to his orgasm as quickly as possible. A truly good sexual experience must be grounded for both the man and his woman in the relationship, in trust, surrender, and lustfulness.

My suggestion is if your man gets extremely excited and ejaculates fast, *make love again* for your pleasure. Creativity eliminates problems.

There is no such thing as "bad technique" between loving humans. "Bad technique" is only having sex for sex's sake.

FEMALE SEXUAL DYSFUNCTIONS

It is obvious to me that feminine-energized women need to be courted, pampered, nurtured, and given affection before they will fully open up. For this to happen, your masculine man must create and lead a sexual experience that is based on tenderness and love for your feelings. When you do not receive that kind of tenderness, it often results in female sexual dysfunction, and the result could be failure to lubricate or inability to achieve orgasm.

I believe this is a woman's unconscious way of saying, "I'm not going to make this easy and pleasurable. I'm going to stay in control in order to be ready to defend myself against your insensitivity, rather than surrender my body to you."

Without affectionate cherishing, men or women may go frigid or become unresponsive, no matter how technically proficient their partner is. Whichever energy you carry into your relationship, your willingness to accommodate your partner's needs must become a priority, or *no sex* may occur.

CHAPTER 16

How to Keep a Sexual Relationship from Turning into an Obsessive Addiction

Dr. James Prescott, formerly of the National Institute of Mental Health, did extensive research on children under the age of two years, who, deprived of being lovingly touched, became adults who were fearful of being touched, and were, therefore, unresponsive to intimacy. If your early years were deficient in healthy affection, as an adult you may be scarred with intimacy and sexual problems of varying degrees.

Human beings need love to survive. To feel safe and responsive as a little girl, you needed to believe that you were accepted unconditionally for yourself.

By the age of three, you decided if love was trustworthy. If you were not well loved, you will probably not be able to bond in a gratifying and satisfying way, physically and/or emotionally to another person. If you don't believe that others really care about you, you will probably seek gratification in the form of food, drink, drugs, anonymous sex, money, power, and prestige as the only options left. Instant gratification will seem right, while long-term relationships will seem dangerous.

For many men and women who are phobic about love due to poor early love training, obsessive, addictive relationships with high levels of pain seem like love. In these cases, therapy and self-help groups like Adult Children of Alcoholics or Codependents Anonymous help people regress to their little child within and finish the process of growing up into a brave adult who can face his or her fears of abandonment and rejection.

Although most of us have some degree of damage that we've had to deal with, sometimes bad relationships overtake the healthiest of us, or we fall into them unknowingly, and when we do, they are like quicksand. We're in deeper and deeper, and before we know it (or want to get out), we're stuck. And, unlike a phobia or some serious childhood scar problem, we stay in them because, as girls, we were taught to think that we could fix things and make them better, or that we had no choice (for who else would love us?), or we could change a man through the power of our love or through our own example. We've all been there at some time, and the best way to handle these awful situations is to use them as a vehicle to grow from.

Have you ever become compulsive when a relationship started to go awry? Most of us have. It starts with a panicky feeling that pushes you into impulsive and compulsive behavior that gets worse and worse until your relationship slowly disintegrates into an addictive one. You are more afraid of the "nothingness" than you are frustrated and resentful, and so you hang on addictively.

How do you know if you are in an obsessive relationship? One sign of an addiction is the reverse side of the original chemical attraction that brought you together. It has been documented that when two people start to come apart, one (or both) partner actually suffers a physical, chemical withdrawal, also known as "lovesickness."

This is, at bottom, a chemical reaction resulting from separation anxiety. Change, for an insecure woman, feels life-threatening and sometimes is.

Have you ever obsessed over a man so much that you called his answering machine just to hear his voice? Or sneaked looks at his credit card bills to see what, or more specifically, whom, he was spending his money on? Sometimes this compulsive behavior becomes so exciting that it ends with pounding on doors, smashing car windows, threats of suicide, or the kind of profound emotional despair that is called clinical depression—all in the name of "love."

But is it love? Remember, a feminine woman doesn't "fall in love." So when a woman "falls in love," what she is really falling into is obsession. To be obsessed with an unavailable man is to be permanently "safe" from receiving an available man's love. It is the "Ghostly Lover" who keeps us mesmerized with the fantasy of perfection at the cost of reality. If you are in the midst of such an obsession and want to end it, you must not taste, touch, smell, see, or hear him for at least two years, and you must date up a storm.

"Self-centered" is feminine. "Selfless" is masculine. Each of us can take on either quality, but we risk addictive behavior when we opt for our second suit in nature, i.e., feminine-energy females who act masculine and go after what they want.

Think and act carefully before you binge. One binge is too many and one thousand binges are not enough for the addictive body.

ADDICTIVE WOMEN

If a woman did not get love and cherishing as a child, particularly from her father, and is desperate to have it, she may later become an addictive personality who finds ways to fill the love void inside. Filling this void becomes the driving force in a dysfunctional girl's life. So a woman must be alert to what she "doesn't want" rather than what she "wants."

The dysfunctional masculine-energy woman goes for money, power, prestige, and independence, and uses men, especially those who are married or unavailable, to gratify her need to appear and feel normal and sexual. However, in reality she rarely is able to surrender to a spiritual sexual love because the loss of independence that is inherent in surrendering to a man is too much for her frightened inner child who feels unprotected and defenseless. This inner child is in need of total control over herself and others, especially sexual men.

Maggie, a tall, blond, beautiful, and successful real estate agent, was just such a woman. Her bright, aggressive style of relating to clients got her what she wanted most—independent money.

Maggie had never married, although she had dated many men. The problem was that each time one of them tried to get her to settle down into a committed relationship, she picked a fight and ended the relationship with no looking back.

Maggie felt lucky that she did not suffer much when she split up with men, as the other women she knew did. She vaguely suspected that it had something to do with her father, whose special little girl she imagined she was, even though he had paid almost no attention to her and, in fact, was cruel and indifferent, even abusive, right up until the day that he left home forever when she was eleven, after a terrible fight with her mother. Maggie never saw or heard from him again.

Maggie became a very pretty girl and was pursued by many boys. When she had sex for the first time, at fifteen, she stopped thinking about her father, and she tried never to look back. But as the years passed and she had no committed relationship in her life, she knew there was a lot she was missing.

By the time she met Kenneth, a married real estate broker in whose firm she began to work, she had just about given up the thought of marriage. Together, the two were very successful and made a lot of money. Then, about eight months after they joined forces, Kenneth began to attempt to seduce Maggie with flowers, presents, and long lunches. Although he was married, eventually he melted her defenses with his affection.

Their lovemaking from the beginning was wonderful for both. Maggie felt safe, secure, open, and uninhibited, unlike her closed defensiveness with the single men she had dated who sometimes accused her of being frigid.

Their affair lasted for three years, during which time they became a real financial team. But then Kenneth began talking about leaving his wife and marrying Maggie. Maggie froze, and as if by some magic switch she began to pull away from Kenneth, feeling smothered and controlled.

Suddenly, Kenneth looked different to her. Everything he did seemed negative, and she began to be sarcastic to him. Their fighting and making up went on for six months, until Kenneth, who had left his family, went back home and refused to deal with Maggie other than coldly in business. He even asked her to leave his office, which she did.

As soon as she left, Maggie wanted him back. The agony drove her to my seminar, where she heard the sad story of the "Amazon Woman" who is trapped in her independent head and cannot sexually open up to an available man. She loves to be with many men, or one man, as long as he is unavailable as Kenneth was.

I worked with her and helped her to see that her childhood loss of Daddy had wounded her badly. Maggie began to keep a journal and read from it to others in her support group. Keeping a journal was mandatory for her. She needed people to hear her pain and know her as a recovering wounded girl. She had to reexperience the pain of loss of her daddy, that agony she had so carefully hidden away.

Finally, Maggie needed to go celibate until she could feel safe with a loving, available man, which she did in her second year of group therapy and individual counseling, when she met and married Ted, a divorced man with one child.

I saw Maggie recently, and she was almost full-term pregnant with their child and was very happy. Her wound was obviously healing, and life was good for the first time.

There is a saying: "It's never too late for a happy childhood."

Fatherless, uncherished girls have the problem of dealing with boundaries in a relationship. As with Maggie, the Amazon Woman's walls are too high and thick.

But for Karen, a "Puella," the walls are nonexistent or too thin to protect her from use and abuse.

When Karen first walked into my office, I saw a pretty, petite, dark-haired woman with a bruise on her well-made-up cheek.

"Please help me. I can't take it anymore," she said, her eyes filling with tears. We began to talk, and a story emerged that was not unusual but serves here as an example of the opposite of Maggie's story.

Karen had really been her daddy's girl. Daddy was a small, sensitive Frenchman; Karen's mama, Frida, was a large, strong Swedish woman.

Karen's relationship with her father was built on fairy tales and songs and walking in the park while he told her about the plants and birds. But Daddy was never well, and he died when Karen was six years old. She lost her only soul mate.

Karen was remarkably docile. She was easily manipulated because she hated to assert herself. The terror she felt at being yelled at or abandoned or rejected was overwhelming. Since her loving daddy died, she had no one in her corner.

When she finished high school, she began working as a hostess in a family restaurant, dating a little but generally staying close to home. Frida worked as a cook in the same restaurant, keeping an eye on Karen, knowing she was an easy mark for any man who could talk her into something. Then one day Mike, a large, robust man ten years older than Karen, came along. Mike was an avid sports fan who owned a barbershop. He drank beer and laughed a lot, and he ate at the restaurant where Karen and her mother worked.

Actually, a better match than Karen and Mike would have been Frida and Mike. They were very similar, but Mike wanted Karen. And Frida wanted Mike in the family one way or another. Although she was neither turned on nor off by him, Karen eventually married him.

It was as if Karen had changed houses but nothing else. She obeyed Mike, did her "duty" sexually, and cared for him. The trouble began when Mike and Karen had been married five years. He had become more prosperous and had bought a second barbershop, but he started drinking too much and fighting with Karen, to the point where he would hit her.

Karen was afraid to leave Mike. She kept her pain inside, relying on God and church and prayer, until one night when Mike came home drunk and began yelling at her. "You're a boring mouse," he said. "I'd rather screw anybody but you."

Somewhere deep inside the rage welled up, and Karen blew. She slammed, ranted, raved, and screamed many years of pain until he backhanded her across the face and stomped out the door.

The next day Karen got my telephone number out of the phone book and came to see me. She talked and cried that day and that night began keeping a journal. She joined a Codependents Anonymous group. She attended my seminars, got a divorce, and moved back in with Frida.

It took time and healing for Karen to eventually move to a little rented house and get back to work at another restaurant. She avoided men like the plague for a couple of years, but eventually she grew into a person who could speak up for herself and set her boundaries.

Karen eventually remarried to a fine man. I did their premarriage counseling, and their marriage is thriving.

LITTLE BOYS WHO POSE AS MEN

As I touched on in Chapter 3, when speaking about giving, women must beware of Little Boys Who Pose as Men.

This is one of the biggest complaints I hear from women who attend my workshops. In therapy I sometimes see a woman hooking up with a man who at first appears to be masculine but in reality is a "Peter Pan" who never got enough love in childhood so that emotionally he hasn't grown up. He becomes a taker who is waiting for "Mom" to arrive.

Real little boys see women, other children, and animals as sources of gratification until they grow up. Then, as men, they become givers, protectors, and cherishers, and view women, children, and animals as recipients of their bounty.

But Peter Pans never reach this stage. Instead, they become womanizing, opportunistic men who feed off needy, addictive, masculine-energy career women. These men do not like to work.

Often a woman can't tell if the man she is with is a real man or a "little boy," because at first Peter Pan acts generous and giving and cherishing of her feelings. He knows that he has to put out to get her to put out.

However, after about four to eight weeks, the generosity ends, and the collection notice arrives. From then on, you're buying his clothes, lending him money, letting him live in your home, and basically paying for his "love" (which is really no more than sex).

Men who magnetize dynamic women know that their job is to be sensuous and sexual while the woman's role is to be financially stable and have some status they can respect.

Some older, rich, or polygamous masculine-energy women like Peter Pans. They are fun and entertaining. Your only problem will be if he finds another '"big mama" with more money and even fewer demands than you.

However, even if he doesn't, a man like this can turn a relationship into a nightmare because usually, after his generous period ends, he will shut down and become passive-aggressive, often deliberately provoking you into begging for him to give you what you want. Little boys love weird women. He sees no problem in driving you crazy, and although you may have been reasonably sane when he met you, he will train you to become weird by pushing you away, then pulling you close again, all within a very short period of time.

So what do you do if you find yourself in such a relationship? You could scream, eat, drink, take drugs, or work obsessively, but I suggest that you say, "I really appreciate what a great guy you are, but I'm not very comfortable here. I'll probably be leaving for the weekend, or permanently."

When she needed insurance for her new car, Joan, a boutique owner, met Carl, a big, good-looking auto insurance salesman.

"I love you," he told her soon after they met. "This is forever." Joan believed him and allowed herself to be swept away by this promise of a lifetime.

At first, their time together was filled with laughter and good times and great sex. Carl was generous and caring, everything Joan wanted in a man. She was living a dream that she hoped would never end.

But as the weeks melted into months, things began to change. "Sweetheart, I'm short this week," Carl said more than once. "Can you lend me some cash? I'll pay it back next week." Joan gave him the money, but next week never came.

One Saturday he came to her house with all of his things. "My landlady is a bitch," he said. "I'm moving in for a few days. All right, love?"

Joan couldn't refuse, and Carl stayed with her for a few weeks, taking full advantage of Joan's kindness and occasionally of the change she left on her dresser.

Then one day she got her phone bill—for $298.00—with all but $50.00 being charges run up by Carl.

When Joan confronted Carl, he acted nonchalant. With a shrug and an air of slight annoyance, he packed quickly, ignoring her tears and demands for repayment. He tweaked her nose just before he gave her a last kiss. "Had fun, sweetheart. See you around sometime," and he was gone.

Joan was devastated and came to one of my seminars to find out what went wrong. I told her she had to learn how to recognize her own needs before a man's. She had to decide whether she wanted to exchange her money for a man's sexual favors, and if not, had to spot "user" males and reject them as soon as possible.

Commitment
(9–12 Months)

CHAPTER 17

Getting Ready for Marriage

Y ou now stand on the precipice of commitment. Behind you stretch the three phases of preparation. Ahead of you are your engagement and marriage. Are you ready to jump?

The Commitment phase rounds out the first year. Like a new spring, this phase provides new life to the relationship and is a foundation for permanence.

After nine months, you've pretty much seen the guy whole cloth. You were in bliss during the Perfect Phase and in despair during the Imperfect Phase, but you've weathered it. You have negotiated the bumps in the Negotiation Period, and you've gotten the best deal you can get with this man. Now you've got to decide whether you want to keep him.

This is the time for both of you to live up to the commitments you have previously negotiated. It is a delicate time, when your diplomacy, strength of constitution, and integrity must come forward. Now, more than ever before, you must be clear about your own intentions and those of the man you love.

REAL LIFE IS NOT A ROMANCE NOVEL

He has told you that he wants to marry you, and you believe him. You are a functioning couple. You have said no to living with him, but you spend most of your time at his place or he at yours. However, as you implement your negotiations about money, space, time, and play styles, you inevitably will have some painful times adjusting to your negotiated terms. I want to prepare you for the pitfalls of this delicate period and arm you with a survival kit, because although it is at this time that you hope everything follows through on course just as in a romantic novel, the truth is that life has many more surprises and quirks than ever found in a novel. For that reason, this is the period I sometimes call "Nine-Month Failure."

GETTING HIM TO PROPOSE

I urge you never to "demand" marriage. I believe it is better for a woman to pass a man up than to demand to be married. I've seen married men in my office—five, ten, twenty years later— who say, "I didn't really choose to marry her. She got pregnant and threatened me, and I married her under duress. I'm still angry about it, and I'm still not committed, and that's the reason that I don't treat her the way she wants to be treated."

You must let him make his own choice. Don't coerce him. Instead of nagging, take a walk. If he wants you enough, he will negotiate. Don't seduce him with money or sexual generosity, and don't try to intimidate him with angry edicts.

Sometimes when a woman is ready to negotiate a (marriage) commitment, she finds that her man isn't. So, how does a feminine woman "manipulate" the situation to move it along—or leave it? It's not easy. As I have said, getting a man often requires a "saintly" amount of patience. A good man is hard to capture, and a woman can't do anything overt to capture him.

Suppose you have a great committed relationship but you have never heard the words from him that specifically say, "Will you marry me?" Many women come to my seminars and say, "Please, how do I get that proposal out of his mouth? I'm feeling so much anxiety."

I assume that if you have been in a relationship from six months to a year, you have had future talk at least in generic terms. For example, you might have said, "It's important for me to be married by the time I am thirty-five, and I'd like to have two children by the time I am forty."

If he has not been direct with asking you for marriage even though it *seems* to be where you are headed, take action. Wait until you are almost to the end of your patience. On a scale of 1 to 10, it would be an 8. This is the time you must speak, because if you wait longer, you will lose your cool and damage or destroy a beautiful relationship.

Pick a pivotal day no longer than eight weeks in the future. If by that day he has not spontaneously come through with a commitment, you must simply say, "I love you. I love being with you. However, I need real commitment in my life. I appreciate the time we have had together, but it is not enough for me to just be together unless we can talk about marriage."

If at this time he cannot, does not, or will not meet your requirement of planning for marriage, you must be willing to let him go.

Think of deep-sea fishing. The only way you are going to get that fish is to get him *on the boat*. On the line is not enough, and the distance between on the line and the boat (marriage) is a long way. It is also in this space between water and boat that you are most likely to lose him. You have to be patient, and the only way you can do that is to be anchored in your own self-love. Because masculine men are more focused logically step-by-step, they are a lot slower than women, who often rationalize away dangers based on feelings, not logic.

WHAT TO DO IF HE'S MADE THE COMMITMENT BUT HE'S DRAGGING HIS FEET

Perhaps he hasn't told his family about your plans to get married, and he has asked you to keep it quiet until he gets the ring (engagement or marriage). Days, weeks, even months go by, and there is mumbling about shopping for "the ring" but *no action*. Or suppose you're both talking about marriage, but his buddies still seem to be as important, or even more important, to him than you are.

Or maybe, even though you are his girlfriend, he suddenly begins to act like a dating bachelor. Perhaps nothing seems different except that the talk about getting engaged has slowed down to a trickle. Maybe, when you ask a question about your future together, he snaps, "Don't pressure me. I'll do it when I'm ready."

There is a cold chill running up your spine. What do you do?

First: *Don't panic.* I will tell you how to handle the man who appears to be avoiding the implementation of your negotiated deal and also help you to discover the truth about his committable or noncommittable nature.

Second: *Don't nag.* Keep quiet until you are prepared to risk losing the deal. At that time, you must be prepared to walk.

Third: *Pick a date* in your head when you are willing to bring on a crisis in your relationship.

Fourth: *Don't have sex, no matter what.* This is the same type of "ultimatum" that is in any contract when it's time to pay up. You tell him you would not be comfortable having sex until he lives up to his commitment. In other words, there are no free lunches or girlfriends.

Fifth: *Keep your composure.* Don't react if he reacts badly to your "ultimatum." State your case, then be quiet. Act like a lady and be patient. Don't argue with him.

Jackie, a city planner, was in love with Dean, a gifted sculptor. Their relationship had been going on for over a year, but Jackie, as she later confessed to me, somehow never felt really secure in it.

Although Dean said he wanted to get engaged, he would never keep a date to go shopping for the ring. There was always a problem finding a time that was convenient for both of them. Finally, Jackie suggested that Dean pick out the ring himself and surprise her.

Time went by and still Dean did not buy her a ring. Jackie began to feel that he was avoiding the whole issue of marriage. She was plagued with feelings of being used and taken for granted. She feared that he had changed his mind about their having a committed future together.

She soon found herself becoming overtly resentful. They began fighting a lot, first about small things and then about bigger things, until one day Jackie screamed at him, "I don't believe you even want this relationship," and Dean, equally angry, yelled back, "Maybe, I don't," and stormed out.

Jackie was in a lot of pain when she came to see me. It was not easy for her to accept that she might have to say good-bye to the man she loved, with whom she had shared dreams, plans, and the investment of a relationship. But I told her that first of all, she must realize and respect that Dean had a right to live his life as he was comfortable. She could not force him to be what she wanted him to be. But even if he was truly in love with her and intended to marry her, these angry outbursts trying to pressure him into action would only push him away, maybe permanently.

I explained, "Dean does what Dean can do. You can only accept or reject but not coerce, or hope foolishly that he will someday change into the prince of your dreams. If he is a frog today, he is going to stay a frog."

Taking my advice on how to set parameters that she would be comfortable with, she approached him and asked if he would be willing to talk about their relationship. I told her to pick a comfortable place and time where interruptions would not occur, and say, "I want to talk to you about our relationship. Is it convenient now or later?" If he said, "Later," she was to wait until then. He agreed on her time to meet, and when they saw each other, she was very centered in her feminine energy.

"I respect your choice," she said, "whatever it may be. However, I am very uncomfortable in this limbo, and until you can make a decision, I feel it's best that we not be sexual."

At first Dean was indignant, claiming that she was trying to coerce him with ultimatums and withhold sex as punishment. He tried to argue that if she withheld sex, she was obviously not in love with him.

"If you really loved me," he said, "you would let things follow their natural course without putting pressure on me."

Remembering my warning about not arguing with him, Jackie simply replied, "I'm sorry, but until you have made a decision, I feel comfortable with a 'no sex' arrangement."

Even when prodded, she refused to be drawn into the trap of an argument. I had carefully explained that since he could stay more logical, he would probably win a rational argument, and she might eventually give in and have sex and therefore spoil him and the relationship.

When Dean left her apartment that night, he was angry. Jackie had trouble sleeping. She wanted to call him and smooth things over, but instead she waited passively, as I had suggested, not getting in touch with him in any way.

Two weeks after her ultimatum, Dean called and asked to see her. He took her out to an expensive new restaurant, but at dinner all he suggested was that they continue as before, letting the future take care of itself. Jackie said she was sorry, but she did not feel comfortable with that arrangement. Dean sulked through dessert, then tried to change her mind again, but Jackie would not be shaken.

They went out a few more times after that. Dean kept telling her he loved her and wanted to be with her, but he did not take any affirmative action, such as buying an engagement ring or setting a marriage date. Jackie held her ground.

Jackie told me she was shaky about what she was doing, but I told her that she must love herself, protect herself, and believe to her core that she deserved the relationship that was right for her. She must be committed and receptive to the right man. I also reminded her that it was the relationship she must commit to, not the person. Dean was a puzzle piece that did not fit. All she could do was keep her end of the bargain. If he didn't keep his, in her own best interest, she had to *move on*.

Each time Jackie saw Dean and he tried to intimidate her or seduce her back into sex, she stood her ground with a smile, even though inside she was in pain.

Then she stopped hearing from him at all, and after eight

weeks of waiting, she began dating again seriously. She went through two more relationships after Dean that aborted between six to ten months. I told her not to be discouraged, and that the right man would come along. Happily, I was proved right. Her relationship with Albert, a successful film editor, went through all the four phases and also lasted more than a year, but when they did marry, Jackie felt extremely solid in the marriage and confident that through her learned negotiation techniques she would be able to deal with whatever problems arose and help the marriage remain viable.

A truly masculine, committed man wants to be generous and responsible, to protect your reputation, and to cherish your feelings about being engaged and married. A selfish man wants freebies. However, a normal man may need to be brought to the awareness that he has begun to act selfishly.

If you are confident in your position, he will be confident in his actions. This confrontation will make him aware that *you love yourself more than you love him.*

You must be careful that you are not harboring old resentments from your communication and negotiation period that were never worked out. If you did not learn these skills well but rather stayed silent and bit your tongue instead of expressing what you did not like and were not comfortable with, you may be expressing a backlog of old angers and resentments. You must reassess your own motivations thoroughly before you write him off as an uncommmittable man.

Jackie learned that she could not intimidate, threaten, or nag Dean into doing his life "her way." She could only relay to her man what she was not willing to live with.

Rhoda and Joe were a committed couple with marriage "somewhere" in the near future.

Rhoda, a secretary at a textile company, was very much in love with Joe, a bartender, and believed he felt the same toward her. However, certain things that she initially thought would change in time continued. For example, Joe's ex-wife was always calling to ask his advice about business, plumbers, and real estate problems, and instead of reminding her that he was no longer her husband, he spent long hours on the phone, helping solve his ex-wife's problems.

Another recurring situation that began to concern her was that Joe kept putting off looking for their apartment. It seemed that there was always a legitimate excuse, but she felt increasingly uncomfortable.

The same was true with their wedding date. He continually delayed setting it. First, it was because his parents needed to be consulted, and they were out of the country. Next he wanted to wait until his promotion at work came through. Then there was some other excuse. Rhoda became distraught, although she said nothing to Joe.

Her mother suggested she come talk with me, which Rhoda was reluctant to do because she felt she would be betraying her faith in Joe. However, she did come, and I soothed her concerns by pointing out that it was out of her love and respect for Joe and their relationship that she needed to deal with the situation clearly.

I told her that she had to remember that marriage means taking on a lot of responsibilities for a masculine man (or woman) and it means a big loss of independence for a feminine woman (or man). Nobody takes these things lightly, and procrastination may be only a defense and not necessarily a refusal to marry.

I helped her realize that what she needed to do in order to help Joe implement his commitment was to set the parameters clearly before him.

When she next talked with Joe, she said, "You know how much I love you and love being with you and planning our future. However, I am feeling uncomfortable about your relationship with your ex-wife, your procrastinating about looking for an apartment, and all the other issues surrounding our engagement and marriage. Because of these things, I will feel better if we become friends until you have thought things through. I respect that you have every right to do what you want about our marriage, including not getting married. But until you have decided what you are going to do about us and *do it*, I don't feel comfortable with us having sex or sleeping together anymore. It would make me feel I was investing in a shaky deal."

I told Rhoda that when Joe demonstrated a positive action, then and only then was she to become sexual again. If he had another attack of procrastination, she must repeat this technique.

Rhoda was worried that he might resent her "ultimatum" and end the relationship. Unfortunately, as I explained to her, there was nothing for her to do but wait eight weeks for him to call. She must not call him or try in any way to make contact with him, and she must not begin a serious sexual relationship with someone else, in case he did come back.

Unlike Dean when Jackie gave her ultimatum, Joe did not resent it, but rather appreciated Rhoda's respect for his right to make a decision. He felt that whatever his choice, it would be *his*. For a committed, masculine man to know that you honor his right to make his own determination about his future is a real turn-on. And if he is not committed, he is not your man.

It is better to know that your relationship is a Nine-Month Failure than to hang on and have it turn into a three- or four-year failure. In fact, you would have to consider the relationship a success, for you have been through the process, and this man has shown his colors and saved you additional wasted time when you could be looking for "Mr. Right." A little pain now is much better than years of it later.

In this case, when Rhoda presented herself with a grounded conviction in her integrity, Joe became more confident about himself and the relationship. After a few weeks he not only politely and firmly cut off his indulgence of his ex-wife, he also set a date for his and Rhoda's marriage and informed the family of this decision.

When it becomes necessary for a woman to take action as Rhoda and Jackie had to do, they can take comfort in the fact that if their man does come back, he will be in charge of himself, which enhances his masculinity. Remember, intimidating your man back or seducing him will not be a good negotiated masculine/feminine commitment.

WHAT ABOUT YOUR FEAR OF COMMITMENT?

If you are with a man who is having trouble following through with his commitment, search yourself and ask if your irritation and resentment may not actually stem from your own resistance to commitment. This may be your way of sabotaging the relationship.

You may not want to give up your independence. As the implementation of the Negotiation Phase grows nearer, you may be rushing to end it rather than be "cool" and let him have the space and time he needs to come around.

Men are not the only ones who fear commitment. Many women fear it as well, and rather than admit this, they explain away their failure to have a permanent relationship by blaming it on uncommittable men.

Her ten months with Miles, the owner of a sporting-goods store, were fun and exciting for Charlene, an advertising executive. She was sure she was in love with him, and he made her feel secure and loved. They did lots of "future talk," discussing children, home life, vacations, and lifestyles. He was supportive of her career in advertising and in general was a mellow and solid man. He had a firm view on the future and the direction he wanted for his life. He was a committable man.

When they reached the Commitment Phase, Charlene began to feel uncomfortable. Life suddenly seemed limited, predictable, and dull. Discussing their fantasies of an ideal relationship in the early part of their relationship had now evolved into their real plans, and Charlene realized that Miles was committing himself to marriage.

Without knowing exactly what she was doing, Charlene began to pull away from Miles. She kept delaying setting the wedding date. It was one thing for her to say, "When we get married someday" and another to circle a date on the calendar. Something was bothering her, but she didn't know what it was.

One day when Charlene had to work late, going over an advertising campaign with Tom, a married TV commercial producer whom she had worked with once before, she found herself saying yes to his suggestion of drinks, yes to dinner, and yes to having sex at his hotel later that night.

Charlene found Tom exciting. He had traveled all over the world making commercials, and he was bright and creative. A clandestine affair began, although Charlene felt disgusted and ashamed of herself because she really believed in a monogamous relationship. She also knew she loved, respected, and valued Miles, but something wouldn't let her give up Tom, even though there was clearly no future with him.

Miles discovered the affair and, in much pain, confronted her. "Why?" he asked.

She could only reply, "I don't know."

Miles had heard about my method of dealing with issues like this and sought my advice. He told me that Charlene was willing to see me, so I agreed to meet with them both in a last attempt to save their relationship.

When I saw Charlene, she admitted that she was afraid of committing herself to a boring life with "Mr. Secure." "Everything is so predictable," she said. "At least with Tom, I never know what is going to happen."

"Well, you know what is not going to happen," I said. "Since he is already married and doesn't want to leave his wife, you are not going to marry Tom."

Charlene was quiet for a moment, and then said, "Maybe that's what I like."

Through our talks, I discovered that Charlene had been through many relationships over the years. These had gotten to the brink of commitment and then fallen apart because she could not go forward. Through our sessions she began to really perceive her lack of commitment. I asked her to decide whether she wanted to remain single and continue to have serial romances with exciting bachelors, or to choose one committable man like Miles and build a marriage.

A committed relationship is not as anxiety-laden as an uncommitted one. It is the chase and capture that are exciting. What Charlene was doing was getting caught in the gratification loop without the cost of commitment or the rewards.

Passion and gratification are seductive, but they are body trips. I wanted her to clearly understand the difference and to carefully analyze her own goals before she made her choice.

Charlene chose to end the affair and continue the relationship with Miles. As her attitude toward commitment changed, Miles again seemed fun. If she had chosen the other path, that, too, would have been fine and her prerogative as long as she was aware of what she was looking for in life.

OLD "BONDINGS" DIE HARD
(CLEARING THE WAY FOR A NEW LOVE)

Sometimes a call from an old relationship can stir up the pain and longings of the unfinished past and make you unsure of your current relationship.

The call from Greg triggered a gut-wrenching light-headed response in Patricia, a vivacious tennis teacher, as it always had, even though she was now in a committed relationship with Howard, a warm and loving businessman. "Hi, hon, it's Greg. I'd like to take you to lunch this week."

Greg, a lawyer who specialized in adoptions, had been the love of her life until he left her for another woman with hardly a good-bye, nearly two years before. Patricia suffered almost a year after he left, during which time she sought me out. She was now grounded in her self-worth and could see Greg in a different perspective. Also, of course, Patricia and Howard were talking about engagement and marriage. Finally, after all the pain of the past, she was beginning a new life, one that was filled with happiness. This meeting with Greg was important to her, and she hoped it would be the severing of the final link between them.

But now, as she heard Greg's voice, she flipped right back into wanting to be with him, and she quickly agreed to meet him for lunch the next day.

As she sat in the restaurant waiting for Greg (he was late, as usual), she had a fantasy in which Greg begged her to give up Howard, and, then, against her will, took her back to his apartment and made crazy, passionate love to her, as in the old days. Then she felt guilty thinking about sex with Greg and switched back to being grounded in her commitment to Howard.

Suddenly, there he was, Greg, the man she had been in love with for so long. Patricia noticed how anxious he appeared as he hugged her, kissed her, and sat down for lunch.

He hardly had time to tell her how beautiful she looked and order a drink before he got down to business.

"Is this thing with Howard serious?" he asked. "You know what a great time we had together. We ought to try again. I have never found another woman like you."

Patricia was silent for a moment. Before, when Greg had left her, she was so devastated, she would have taken any part of him she could get. Her days and nights were filled with the fantasy of his returning and begging her to take him back. But those days of self-abuse were gone.

"Greg," she said, "when you left, I was devastated. It took me almost a year to get over you, and the scars were very deep. I don't ever want to put myself through that kind of pain again. Howard is a really good man. I love him, and we are planning to be married. I appreciate your asking me, but I am committed to my relationship with Howard."

Patricia was brave to go back rather than let the "Ghostly Lover" haunt her. In such a situation, you must strive to develop an empathy for your ex-lover by saying, "I am glad you're successful in your work," or "I'm glad you've found someone to love." Through this you can set yourself free and be ready to commit to someone else.

WAIT A YEAR TO MARRY

Of course, not everyone is uncommittable or gets cold feet or fantasizes about the past. Sometimes you and he are totally in sync and want nothing more than to marry and settle down together. That's wonderful, as long as you wait a year to marry so you can really know whom you are with.

No one can know anyone else until at least four seasons have passed. Someone who might be fun in the summer might change totally with the cold weather. There is even a neurological impairment called SAD (Seasonal Affect Disorder), in which the amount of light a person takes in can impact on brain chemistry and create depression, which you and he would have to deal with.

Alisha, a designer, knew Jim only three months when she married him. It was a whirlwind courtship, and their attraction was intense and immediate. Jim, a wealthy businessman, took her to expensive restaurants and bought her lavish gifts. When he proposed, Alisha accepted, and they slipped away to Monterey and were married by a local justice of the peace. It was a beautiful sunset ceremony on a bluff overlooking the ocean.

Almost immediately, things changed. Alisha found that after marriage, Jim became financially stingy and was deeply in debt. He found her demanding and spoiled, a pampered little princess who wanted to redesign him in the image of her industrialist father. They began to bicker; then the fights accelerated, and after short time they hated each other, and a bitter divorce ensued.

Rushing into a lifetime commitment is like playing a crap game with your future. Surely, you would not buy a house without first checking out the electrical wiring, plumbing, roof, and title clearance. I urge you to love yourself enough to spend the time to get to know your prospective mate, and he you. Work through my four phases and go into marriage as a strong, united couple. You deserve that.

NEGOTIATE A ROLE CHANGE

Earlier, in the Perfect Phase of your relationship, you discovered that despite the fact that you are a complex "ambisexual" human being, in order to have a successful relationship you had to choose either to be the generous, protective, cherishing "male," or the receiving, responsive, available "female." Then, in the negotiation chapter, you learned how to begin to negotiate for some changes in your new role, changes that allowed each of you to take charge of areas you felt confident in or relinquish ones you didn't, with the permission of your mate.

Now, at the Commitment Phase, when you both understand and are comfortable in your own energy *preference* and that of your partner, the courtship has been grounded in a long-term relationship, and you are ready to think about legalizing it, you are now both free to express both your masculine and your feminine energies. This is the time when the "switch" should occur naturally and with ease. However, the same principle holds now as in the early stages of your relationship. Only one type of energy at a time is successful. If you are predominantly feminine but choose for the moment to be masculine, your partner must complement you by switching to feminine, and vice versa. Otherwise collision occurs that can undo the relationship, especially in its delicate first year.

There are no taboos or parameters in terms of role switching as the relationship grows older. It is all negotiable according to need. The only requirement is to signal a role change through communication. "I have an idea. Do you want to hear it?" or "I have some painful feelings. Will you listen?"

The beginning of a relationship has a predominant male-energy person and a predominant female-energy person. As time goes by they meld together in a waltz of compatibility and communication of thoughts and feelings. A breadwinner still may opt to be female while a "little woman" or "Mr. Mom" is really male. Communication, not tasks, indicates maleness and femaleness.

One of the wonderful things about the Commitment Phase is that you both get to be masculine, and you both get to be feminine. There is a predominant leader and follower, but eventually the follower will sometimes be the leader, and the leader will sometimes follow. In a mutual exchange, there are times when each will be cherished and respected.

But this happens only when you can communicate verbally,

and negotiate, which to me is the highest form of love. Remember that according to Dr. Carl Jung every smart man is also a sensitive woman, and every sensitive woman is also a smart man. Complexities must be dealt with in every intimate relationship.

How to do this? It is not difficult. You need only signal your partner that you wish to "switch" energies.

If you are predominantly masculine energy (the pursuer) and you wish to speak about your negative feelings, you begin by saying, "I have some negative feelings I want to share with you. Are you willing to listen?"

By doing this, you switch from masculine to feminine. Your partner now becomes the masculine energy, giving and cherishing your feelings.

If you were the original feminine energy (the pursued), you can always share negative feelings and vetoes freely, but when you wish to become masculine, you can change roles by saying, "I have an idea (opinion, suggestion, want) that I'd like to share with you. Are you willing to listen?"

Being flexible gives both of you a way to communicate your thoughts, wants, feelings, and vetoes.

Learn to let the energies flow between respect and cherishing. Just remember that there are only two thrones, one for the king, one for the queen, and that each throne can accommodate only one person at a time.

NEGOTIATE AND RENEGOTIATE

During the Negotiation Phase, you learned how to approach each other and express your likes and dislikes with skill and positive diplomacy. With these techniques, you moved to the Commitment Phase with success. But even after implementing the commitment by becoming engaged or getting married, you must continue to use these negotiation skills as a natural part of your relationship.

Engagement and marriage are not the end goal of commitment but rather the beginning. To keep your commitment viable, you must use your negotiation skills throughout your relationship. Everything remains negotiable and is continually renegotiated because nothing in life is constant, even among successful people.

In Hollywood I see it all the time. Last year, Betty was a waitress/actress hoping for a hundred dollars a week in tips. This year, she is making eight thousand dollars a week on a TV series. The question is not just who is the main breadwinner now. *Masculine energy and feminine energy are not connected to the amount of money earned, but how it is handled and by whom.*

Assuming Betty was "feminine" before she was successful, she could decide that she is now the masculine energy and assert herself accordingly. Or she may remain the feminine energy and let her man continue to handle the income and investments.

It could also happen that one of the partners backtracks on a nonnegotiable item. This was the case in the relationship between Wanda and her fiancé, Barry.

Wanda, a secretary for a shoe company, moved in with Barry, her boss, after he gave her an engagement ring. They had previously agreed that they wanted a baby as soon as they married, but two months before the ceremony was to take place, Wanda found out she was pregnant. Thrilled with the news, she waited to tell Barry over dinner that evening. But Barry's response was anything but joyful. "Why weren't you more careful?" he snapped. "How could this have happened?"

Wanda was devastated and near tears. "I guess I forgot one of my pills," she said. "But what does it matter? I thought we agreed to have a baby right away. Are you telling me you don't want it?"

"I want a baby when I decide to have one," Barry said angrily. "Not by accident."

Wanda was hurt and in pain. How could she have felt so secure one moment and so alone the next? Silence dominated the rest of the evening. They could hardly communicate on even the daily, mundane things.

That night Barry slept in the extra bedroom, and for the next few days they were cool and distant, both at home and at the office. Both had their own agendas. Barry hoped Wanda would give in and abort the unwanted pregnancy. He had a plan for their first baby, and this wasn't it. He felt trapped, as if he had had no part in the deal. Wanda, however, was not about to give in and have an abortion. Although she had perhaps been irresponsible in not following the calendar carefully, their commitment was to have a baby as soon as possible after marriage. Barry had reneged on a nonnegotiable item for her—a child.

As the days went by and Wanda held firm to her convictions, Barry thought about the situation and soon realized that his feeling of not being in control of events was far outweighed by his commitment to her and their life together.

Barry approached her sheepishly with flowers in hand. "Wanda, honey," he said, "I've made a mistake in reacting so badly. I love you, both of you, and of course I want this baby. It's ours."

As Barry took Wanda into his arms, she realized that by standing her ground and not arguing, she was able to make Barry understand that she loved herself and the baby more than she loved Barry, and that he must accept that or lose them both.

In the long haul of marriage, your self-love will form an anchor in a stormy sea and a spiritual bedrock for your home. When a woman loves her man better than herself, she runs the risk of being used and abused. *Don't do it!*

A very serious dilemma occurs when a nonnegotiable item is reneged on *after* marriage.

For example, although Justin was an upwardly mobile attorney, he married Lorraine, a coat designer, thinking that even after the babies came, she would continue to work. He felt that her income would enhance the quality of their life. Although she had committed to this course, once she had her second baby, she wanted to stay home and be a full-time mommy. This added to his burden, by making him their sole source of support.

Another example would be a man and woman who agree

before marriage that they want children, but afterward he keeps putting it off and then decides he doesn't want them after all, or even confesses that he actually never did want them.

To stay together today, a couple has to negotiate and renegotiate continuously, and that is the way it should be. If the negotiation table is not available and actively used, they could start to take each other for granted, which in itself can be the kiss of death.

PART FOUR

THE REST OF
THE STORY

CHAPTER 18

For the Rest
of Our Lives

Between the ages of forty and sixty, hormones switch for all of us. It's when men become women and women become men.

What I mean is that after the age of fifty, when you are in menopause and your estrogen level drops, the progesterone will begin to impact on you. You will be more thought-oriented and less feeling-oriented than you were earlier. You will be able to deal well with the push and shove of business. You won't need, at this point, to be the loving mom anymore, because usually the kids are grown. It is very valuable for a woman of a certain age, with her progesterone-based system, to go out into the world and make her mark. Now is her time.

As a man ages, his testosterone level drops, and he becomes influenced by the estrogen in his body. Because a man will be more feeling-centered than he was previously, he cannot be expected to be as performance-oriented as he was. I usually find that the older man is kinder than the younger one, and the older woman is often crabbier than the younger one, because estrogen, wherever it is, likes to feel good. So, for a woman, it's during her youth, and for a man, it's his maturity.

A woman makes a grave mistake when she does not help her mature man relax into his feelings. This is the time when he wants to do the gourmet cooking and she wants to go back to school.

If a feminine-energy woman requires a man to stay an over-achieving, money-making, problem-solving, masculine male all of his life, she risks losing him because she is asking him to overextend himself to the point of stress, which can be a cause of heart disease and other chronic, disabling illnesses.

A man must learn to be more like a woman. Eventually, he must kick back, retire, go back into a pleasure-centered world, and stop making the last buck on the planet. And after mid-life, women must stop seeing themselves as total recipients of a man's generosity. They must start taking responsibility.

Menopause is now being delayed. It used to occur most often around age forty-five, but now it usually arrives at about age fifty-two. Women are having children later, because women are younger than they were. A forty-year-old woman is now the way a thirty-year-old woman used to be.

Communication techniques and assumptions must switch with the mature couple. Where formerly he was expected to know what he thought and what he wanted, now she must know, as an older woman, what she wants and what she thinks. As a young man, he used to take care of her. Now, in their maturity, she must take care of him.

Whereas earlier the initiative right was his and the veto right was hers, in mid-life those rights switch.

Now, in maturity, she must know what she thinks and wants, but she must also listen to her man. She must be able to cherish him, because he is now in his "feelings" phase.

So she says, "How do you feel about retiring, or moving here or there?" and he will tell her and she will listen.

With an age gap, problems do arise. When he is older and she is younger, *both* are biologically female. They must negotiate *over* the biological urge to receive pleasure. When she is older and he is younger, they must negotiate *over* the biological urge to control the other.

Here is a pledge I ask all the women at my seminars who are over forty to take:

"I PROMISE TO CHERISH THE FEELINGS OF MY OLDER MAN, EVEN WHEN HE IS ILLOGICAL, IRRATIONAL, AND OFTEN IRRITATING."

Of course, there's one for the men over forty as well:

"I PROMISE TO RESPECT THE WOMAN IN MY LIFE, EVEN WHEN I KNOW I USED TO BE SMARTER."

So, the point of this process is first, that you know yourself. Know what principle, or energy system, you are carrying into the relationship, but be prepared to make changes to ease the relationship into its Golden Years. And second, that you allow the other person to be the opposite of you so that you work together in equity to exchange your energy systems. You get into trouble only when you duplicate systems. You do not get into trouble when you complement them.

CHAPTER 19

Ten Secrets for Getting and Keeping the Right Man

1. Choose to Be Respected or Cherished.

    You've got to know who you are before you can exchange
    what you've got. In every relationship, there can be only
    one respected leader and one cherished follower, at least
    in the beginning until a commitment has been negotiated.
    Choose whether you want to be the giving/male or the
    receiving/female, regardless of your anatomy. Whatever
    you choose, have integrity.

2. Pay Attention to Your Feelings.

    Always pay attention to your feelings. Avoid what you
    don't want. Feminine energy must feel good to do good.
    (Masculine energy must do good to feel good.) Don't ra-
    tionalize away negative feelings, no matter who tells you
    to. If it doesn't feel good, don't do it. Honor your body.

3. Flirt to Attract.

    If you want to "attract" a male, you must be "seen" as a sex
    object. Take care of your body, dress sensuously, fix your
    hair and makeup, go where men are, catch "his" eye, and
    signal your interest and availability (the Five-Second Flirt
    Technique) so he won't be afraid to approach you. Smile,
    don't talk. If you speak first, you're the better man.

4. You Need Chemistry, Compatibility, and Communication.

You need all three, but they don't have to be perfect. Chemistry is a body-to-body reaction. Enjoy it, but don't consummate too soon. Communicate first to investigate compatibility, in order to separate your fantasy projection from reality. He could be crazy, married, or a "little boy." Once the bodies take over, it's hard to negotiate compatibility or even learn to communicate.

5. Have No Sex Without Commitment.

Most females become bonded to the male with whom they have a sexual relationship, so unless you're "man" enough for casual sex, negotiate the commitment before making love. Find out in advance whether he'll pay the "entrance fee," which is exclusivity, continuity, and longevity. Remember, men fall in love with your virtue, not your body.

6. Set Aside Fifteen Minutes a Day to Talk.

Every day, each of you should do "Amigo Talk," asking the other what he or she thinks and feels about things that matter to you. Learn how to help the other to feel better and to achieve his or her goals. Then each of you should try to execute your tasks. When a man's thinking is respected, he feels cherished. When a woman's feelings are cherished, she feels respected.

7. Renegotiate Terms Regularly After Six Months.

The first three months are the Perfect Phase, the next three the Imperfect Phase. At six months you start negotiating time, space, play, and money, and at nine months, the Commitment period, you begin planning for the future. You must renegotiate regularly to accommodate changes and to give both partners the variety of switching roles.

8. Keep All Agreements.

The only way you know you love yourself and others is by the agreements you are willing to make and keep. Respect and cherish each other daily. Don't give up unless he makes you sick or drives you crazy. Nobody is perfect. If he's 51 percent, keep him.

9. Create a Romantic Memory Bank.

A romantic memory is one in which the male gives pleasure to you, and you give pleasure back to him (but always a little less than you get). When the male is giving, protecting, and cherishing, he is penetrating your defenses so that you can surrender to the pleasure of the relationship. You must never ask a man for more, better, or different love, so pick a male who gives the way you like to receive.

10. Wait at Least a Year to Marry.

You don't know a person until you've been through four seasons with him. You must each have accepted the other's foibles and frailties. The male must know what he thinks and ask for what he wants. The female must know what she feels and what she doesn't want and say no to anything unethical or immoral. You have negotiated time, space, money, and play. If you must marry or sign papers sooner than a year, make sure you seek legal counsel first.

CHAPTER 20

Questions and Answers from the Floor

Q. My parents never talked to me about sex, except to tell me, "No intercourse before marriage." Of course I rebelled and had sex anyway. However, I still have a problem about thinking sex is dirty, which causes me to be frigid and not enjoy and want sex. Now I've met a man I really like, and I'm in conflict. Help!

A. Please come to therapy. We can do things to unscramble Mom and Dad in your head.

Q. I have a question about oxytocin. Are there women who do not get bonded to a man by sex?

A. Yes, there are masculine-energy women who can intellectually override their biological reaction to bonding physically to a sexually pleasuring male. They can have as many lovers as they want and not get bonded.

These women run their lives through their heads and not their bodies. They simply do not feel sex like a sensitive woman and will not relax and bond unless they respect the man, his career, and his leadership abilities. It is a "mind over matter" thing.

Q. I had sex with a man who said he was crazy about me, after getting a contract for longevity, monogamy, and continuity. But then he pulled away for two weeks.

When I finally confronted him, he told me that he had freaked out because I did some things that reminded him of his ex-girlfriend. We decided that we would try again and communicate more openly, but I've noticed that the more I talk, the quieter and more distant he becomes. What is going on? Do you think he was lying to me to get me to go to bed with him?

A. He is probably not finished with his ex-girlfriend. Often relationships split up prematurely and the negative residue shows up in the next relationship. He is tying all those unresolved issues into your relationship as a defense against committing and being vulnerable.

Committable men and women realize that each relationship and person is separate and unique. Even when the relationship doesn't work out, they are brave and can take new risks. But uncommittable people won't risk. They shut down at the first sign of trouble. Leave him alone and don't give him sex as a "Band-Aid" transitional relationship.

Q. My boyfriend recently left me. He said I make him feel inadequate because I have a better job and make more money than he does. How can I get him back?

A. He left because he was in "male-to-male" competition with you. In his head, you were more respectfully masculine than he was, and he blamed you for it.

Inadequate men are so angry at a woman's abilities and success that they will leave her for a woman who has less so they can feel adequate. You have two choices. You can either find a sensitive man who is secure enough to respect your accomplishments, or you can throw away your career and keep your boyfriend. My advice is to find another man. You can always replace a man, but not yourself.

Q. How do you know when a man is really in love with you?

A. There are three ways to know. One, he will be generous with his body, with his mind, and with his money. Two, he will want to be protective of you, so he won't call you up at three o'clock in the morning to say, "C'mon over, honey, I need to get laid." And three, he will put your feelings ahead of his own. If he puts his own feelings ahead of yours, he's not a man, he's a little boy.

Q. How do you know if he is the "right" person?

A. There are no "right" people. There's a right person for right now. And chances are the one right in front of your face is right. We have multiple choices. If you miss one now, someone else will show up.

   Very often what's right for you today isn't right for you tomorrow. So marriage is a difficult thing. It takes a lot of luck to stay with someone for the long haul.

Q. You say we are all masculine and respectable at work. Then how do I get a man I meet at work to see me as a feminine woman and ask me out?

A. Act like Clark Kent. Switch from Superwoman to a feminine woman during coffee breaks, lunch hours, happy hours, or office parties. Don't start talking about business outside of business hours. In fact, stop talking. Use eye contact and smiles, and let him speak first. Then listen. Silence is golden and magnetic. Let him lead and chase you for a date.

Q. I'm single and have been having an affair for two years with my married boss. He tells me he is in love with me but can't leave his wife until his fifteen-year-old son graduates from high school. Should I believe him and wait?

A. Only if you don't want to get married, and you also believe in fairy tales. You are being used as a "side dish" to pepper up his sagging marriage. Is this what you want? Do you like your independence enough not to get married?

Q. I had some painful experiences in the past and am afraid to trust and commit to a man.

A. You are right not to trust men. You shouldn't trust anyone until after you get to know that person and he (or she) has proved to be *trustworthy*. Remember, we are all broken and defective and therefore not worth committing to. When you relate to a man on an intimate basis, you are saying to yourself, "I'm going to find out where he is defective, and see if *I* can handle it."

So never commit to a man. Commit to the relationship. Trust that you're going to handle the defects of his character, and have faith that you will be able to handle yourself when he does things that cause you pain. Because that's what commitment is made of. You carry your end of the game and see if he carries his.

Q. Is it okay to marry a younger man?

A. Definitely. Often a powerful woman will find that the men her age are too competitive with her because they feel inadequate. An inadequate man may attempt to chop her down to size. Often a woman like this will go for men either ten to fifteen years older or ten to fifteen years younger, or for a European man. I have found that European men are not as afraid of women as men in our culture are, because Europe is a patriarchal society, while in America women have a powerful hold on child-rearing, because of the preponderance of men who abandon their families.

Q. How do you fight with a man?

A. You don't. You say, "You know, honey, you may be right that it was Friday, or Tuesday, or that my mother was there. That's not the way I recall it, but it doesn't matter. It's not worth fighting over." If you do this, I can promise you that within sixty minutes he will be back saying, "You know what? I've thought about it. You may be right."

A masculine man does not want to fight with a vulnerable woman. He doesn't want to win, unless you act like a man. If a man wants to fight, he goes to war. When he comes home, he wants to play with you.

Does that mean you're a "nebbish"? No. It means that when he tells you what he thinks and what he wants, he asks you how you feel about it and he takes those feelings into account and you tell him the absolute truth. Remember what Grandma did. She'd say, "Oh, Grandpa" and roll those eyes because she knew if she kept Grandpa happy, he wouldn't die on her, or leave her for a bimbo who didn't know how to add one plus one.

Q. How do you look like you want to get married?

A. You do it by looking like you want to get "laid," because that's the beginning of getting married. Men see a woman they want to have sex with, and then it's a matter of negotiating the cost factor. For some women, it's a dinner. For others it's two hundred bucks on the bed right now. At least prostitutes are smart enough to get the money up front.

   So if you want to get married, look as though you want to play. Be receptive, available, vulnerable, approachable, lovable, and sexual.

Q. I recently met a new man. I don't know if marriage is necessarily a goal for either of us, but I want the opportunity of sexually exploring this relationship without having to get bonded. Is this possible?

A. Not if you're the "female" in the relationship. If you're the female, you do have to know up front if marriage is a possibility, because you probably will bond with him.

   Only if a man says, "I'm not opposed to marriage. I may not marry you, but I want a monogamous relationship," can you take a chance on him. Of course, sometimes, in the heat of the moment, a man might say he wants marriage but then will later take it back and admit that he was talking impulsively. Very often the penis and the brain get confused, and in that case, two heads are not better than one.

Q. I am a forty-year-old single woman. I have just lost the man I have loved for twenty years. He was the only one I ever wanted. I want to get married, but I'm too frightened, and I feel too old to try again. What should I do?

A. If you really feel that way, I recommend that you stay single. There is no security and stability in life. If you are looking for the illusion of security and stability, you are still a child waiting for Mommy and Daddy to come and be Santa Claus. They're not coming, and neither is Santa Claus.

   The greatest lives are built on the greatest fiascoes. Security and stability equal stagnation. If you want to live to the fullest, get out there and make as many creative mistakes as possible.

Here's an antisecurity, antistability pledge:

"I PROMISE ON MY HONOR TO CREATE AS MANY MISTAKES AS I CAN, FOR I SHALL LEARN FROM THEM AND LIVE A FULL AND EXCITING LIFE."

Q. I am thirty years old and single, and I have been seeing a man for almost three months whom I thought I was madly in love with. My feelings have suddenly changed drastically. I want to end the relationship, but I am confused as to why. I think it's because I earn more money than he does, and I'm not willing to wait for him to find financial success.

A. There are career women, and there are women with a career. If you cherish your career more than the man you are in love with, then that is your right and choice.

Q. I am very much in love with a man who when he drinks alcohol becomes very different and unbearable. What should I do?

A. When a man uses alcohol or drugs, he is trying to knock out his rational brain and to climb down into his feminine impulsive gut in order to give himself permission to do stupid things.

If you like being the thinking woman who cherishes her man through thick and thin, take care of him. If you like being a cherished woman with a thinking man, avoid drunks. Go to some Al-Anon meetings and see other women dealing with this issue.

Q. What happens when a woman drinks or uses drugs?

A. It's the opposite of what happens with a man. When a woman uses drugs or alcohol, she is attempting to knock out her feelings in order to climb up into her rational brain to do stupid things, such as marrying stupid people or staying in stupid jobs that don't feel good.

Q. I'm thirty-two and divorced. I've been in a relationship with a terrific guy for six months, but now he has pulled back. He says he is stuck and can't move forward in the relationship. Still, he keeps calling and writing. What should I do to get things back on track?

A. When a man says, "I don't know what I want, but I need space," you say, "I'll wait, but while I wait, I'll continue to date others." That should move him. If not, move on.

Q. I am in a relationship with a man who is very loving, cherishing, and giving. But when I become responsive and try to move the relationship forward, he pulls away.

A. When you try to move the relationship forward, you are not responding, you are taking charge. If you were responsive, you would say, "Yes, please," and "Thank you." He is the man, and you do it his way and in his time frame. If you ask him for more or better love, time, affection, or sex, he will usually pull away and give you less.

Q. I have been in a relationship for seven months in which I am the masculine energy and he is the feminine. Is it possible to change the dynamics so he will be the masculine one and I will be the feminine? I'd like to give him "balls."

A. Women can't give men "balls." They either grow them or own them themselves, but you can't give them to your man.

Why don't you ask him what he wants and what he thinks, and tell him what you feel and what you don't want. That way you can just drop your "balls," and perhaps he'll pick his up.

Q. I am interested in dating a man who is in the process of getting divorced. Is that okay?

A. A man is married when he signs a legal document and divorced when he signs the divorce papers. Anything in between means he is still married.

Q. Aren't men afraid that a woman may fall in love with someone else if they let weeks go by before they call again?

A. Yes. That's why they usually call in six to eight weeks in order to stop her leaving. If you call, he is safe, and you are not. If you don't, you are safe, and he is not. Be patient! Wait!

Q. How can I get over an obsession with a man who is emotionally unavailable? I see him all the time, and the obsession is affecting all my other relationships.

A. To be obsessed with an unavailable man is to be permanently safe from receiving from an available one. The "Ghostly Lover" keeps us mesmerized with the fantasy of perfection at the cost of reality. The way to get over him is to stay away. Don't taste, touch, smell, see, or hear him for two years, and in the meantime, date up a storm.

Q. Recently I have started seeing a man I like very much. He says and does all the right things. He talks about longevity, continuity, and exclusivity; he is extremely generous, he cherishes my feelings, and we have a lot of fun together. He has taken the physical part very slowly—lots of hugging and touching. I'd like to continue this relationship, but how and when do I tell him that I carry the herpes virus?

A. Before sex. It is illegal in many states to keep such information from him. If he has a nonnegotiable item about herpes, he will be gone safely and quickly. If herpes is a negotiable item, he will work with you and your doctor. Tell him as soon as possible for the sake of your own comfort.

Q. I've been seeing a married man on and off for four years. Although I'm fond of him and enjoy his company, I have no desire to marry him because he is much younger than I. I thought it would be nice to have him around until the right man comes along. Am I fooling myself?

A. You may be one super dude of a guy who can have casual

sex like the guys. As I've said, there are women like that. On the other hand, you have inadvertently bonded to this man, and you don't realize it. All I can tell is that for the past four years you've been casually connected to this guy, and I don't see you doing anything else.

Beware of whom you have sex with. Your body may fall in love with a man who is wrong for you. Falling in love is called *bonding*.

THE BEST KIND OF MARRIAGE

For marriage to be a success, I believe it must be a "covenant" formed by a feminine-energy person who is grounded in his or her worthiness and desirability and by a masculine-energy person who is grounded in his or her competence and adequacy. Feminine energy is magnetic to the masculine energy's dynamic self, which is generous and giving to the feminine energy who requires receiving first, before giving back.

So the feminine energy and the masculine energy get together and form a grounded relationship in which they negotiate a mutual interdependency and become a balanced unit in the world for a greater good. This "greater good" is their love, their spirituality, and this, not just gratification alone, is their goal in life.

If they don't have purpose for their relationship, gratification won't hold it. There has to be more than pleasing each other's bodies. Life seeking gratification rarely has much love, but life seeking love has a great deal of gratification. The body can never really be satisfied; only the soul can be satisfied.

Two people in a covenant maintain a lot of autonomy. They stay themselves. They have their own friends, their own interests. They share themselves, and they negotiate the deal. These people make a difference in the world. Their way of relating demonstrates the spiritual good in a relationship, and the interesting thing is that this relationship gets better and better and better. These are the people who can be together through thick and thin, money and no money, health and illness, because what they are really doing is loving. And these are the people who love the best because they love the other person as well as themselves.

Nobody needs a piece of paper to get married. The marriage really starts when the masculine energy gives up his or her birthright of polygamy, and the feminine risks being bonded by giving his or her body. But I believe that if you want 100 percent commitment with all the doors shut, the physical, the mental, and the emotional, you must be married legally. It is your commitment to society. When a man commits on paper, he is *committed*.

In marriage, bodies commit sexually and sensually. The mind commits with money and property and status in the community. When the body and the mind are committed, you have Like, Love, and Lust, and then and then only then is the person "in love."

To love and be loved is the ultimate spiritual goal of all good people. May you find your man, build a solid foundation, and reap the rewards of a loving marriage.

If my book succeeds in getting you there, you still have to understand that life is a process, and that our marriages, the way we live together, the way we communicate, and the way we negotiate all must change as we do.